C000069816

(

Grete Anton

Carriage of Goods by Sea

UNCITRAL Draft Instrument on Carriage of Goods by Sea and the Possibility of Harmonization of Carrier Liability Regimes

LAP LAMBERT Academic Publishing

Impressum/Imprint (nur für Deutschland/ only for Germany)

Bibliografische Information der Deutschen Nationalbibliothek: Die Deutsche Nationalbibliothek verzeichnet diese Publikation in der Deutschen Nationalbibliografie; detaillierte bibliografische Daten sind im Internet über http://dnb.d-nb.de abrufbar.
Alle in diesem Buch genannten Marken und Produktnamen unterliegen warenzeichen-, marken- oder patentrechtlichem Schutz bzw. sind Warenzeichen oder eingetragene Warenzeichen der jeweiligen Inhaber. Die Wiedergabe von Marken, Produktnamen, Gebrauchsnamen, Handelsnamen, Warenbezeichnungen u.s.w. in diesem Werk berechtigt auch ohne besondere Kennzeichnung nicht zu der Annahme, dass solche Namen im Sinne der Warenzeichen- und Markenschutzgesetzgebung als frei zu betrachten wären und daher von jedermann benutzt werden dürften.

Coverbild: www.ingimage.com

Verlag: LAP LAMBERT Academic Publishing AG & Co. KG
Dudweiler Landstr. 99, 66123 Saarbrücken, Deutschland
Telefon +49 681 3720-310, Telefax +49 681 3720-3109
Email: info@lap-publishing.com

Herstellung in Deutschland:
Schaltungsdienst Lange o.H.G., Berlin
Books on Demand GmbH, Norderstedt
Reha GmbH, Saarbrücken
Amazon Distribution GmbH, Leipzig
ISBN: 978-3-8383-7165-8

Imprint (only for USA, GB)

Bibliographic information published by the Deutsche Nationalbibliothek: The Deutsche Nationalbibliothek lists this publication in the Deutsche Nationalbibliografie; detailed bibliographic data are available in the Internet at http://dnb.d-nb.de.
Any brand names and product names mentioned in this book are subject to trademark, brand or patent protection and are trademarks or registered trademarks of their respective holders. The use of brand names, product names, common names, trade names, product descriptions etc. even without a particular marking in this works is in no way to be construed to mean that such names may be regarded as unrestricted in respect of trademark and brand protection legislation and could thus be used by anyone.

Cover image: www.ingimage.com

Publisher: LAP LAMBERT Academic Publishing AG & Co. KG
Dudweiler Landstr. 99, 66123 Saarbrücken, Germany
Phone +49 681 3720-310, Fax +49 681 3720-3109
Email: info@lap-publishing.com

Printed in the U.S.A.
Printed in the U.K. by (see last page)
ISBN: 978-3-8383-7165-8

Table of contents

Abbreviations

CMI – Comité Maritime International

ECT – Treaty Establishing European Community

EEC – European Economic Community

EU – European Union

Hague Rules – International Convention for the Unification of Certain Rules of Law relating to
        Bills of Lading

Hague-Visby Rules – The Hague Rules as Amended by the Brussels Protocol 1968

Hamburg Rules – United Nations Convention on the Carriage of Goods by Sea, 1978

IMF – International Monetary Fund

SDR – Special Drawing Right

TEU – Treaty on European Union

UN – United Nations

UNCITRAL – United Nations Commission on International Trade Law

UNCITRAL D.I. – The UNCITRAL Draft Instrument on the carriage of goods [wholly or
        partly][by sea]

UNCTAD – United Nations Conference on Trade and Development

Rules – any of the existing International Conventions on carrier liability (the Hague Rules,
    Hague-Visby Rules and Hamburg Rules) but also the UNCITRAL Draft Instrument on
    carriage of goods [wholly or partly][by sea]

Relevant definitions

Consignee	Person entitled to take delivery of the goods under a contract of carriage or a transport document or electronic record. Definition by United Nations Commission on International Trade Law's Draft Instrument on the carriage of goods [wholly or partly][by sea]
Freight forwarder	A person or company whose business is to receive and ship goods for others. Also termed forwarding agent. See Black's Law Dictionary for more information!
Indorsee	The person in whose favor a negotiable document is made, or assigned by indorsement. Also spelled endorsee. See Black's Law Dictionary for more information!
Intermodal transport	Combines at least two modes of transport (road, rail, water, air), usually in the way that combines the advantages of each mode of transport. A smart solutions for shipping containerized goods. Also termed multimodal transport.
SDR	Special Drawing Right is an international reserve asset created by the IMF in 1969. Value based on basket of key international currencies. Serves as unit of account of the IMF and some other international organizations. See IMF's Website for more information! <http://www.imf.org/external/np/exr/facts/sdr.htm>
Seaworthiness	An implied obligation on the shipowner to provide a vessel that is capable of performing the journey referred to in the contract of carriage. Also includes cargoworthiness (the ship is capable of carrying the cargo in question), appropriate equipment and competent crew capable of dealing with ordinary perils of the sea.

A Introduction

Trade is the cornerstone of economy. Carriage of goods by sea is one of the oldest exercises of private international law – shores of a sea generally tend to be divided between several states. We're on the height of globalisation – vast quantities of goods are carried by sea every day. Sea transport in the European Union accounts for an impressive percentage of the overall transport. It is difficult to say whether arrangements that have worked for decades (or even centuries) have become inadequate due to technological process, whether the problems have always been waiting for a solution and the time is finally right, or whether the demands have grown, but finally an attempt towards harmonization of carrier liability has commenced.

In my thesis I am going to describe the present situation, explain how the existing Carrier Liability Conventions are interrelated, what the liability Regimes evolved from, what sort of solutions the current situation requires and what factors will need to be taken into consideration to achieve that aim. I am also looking at maritime law in Estonia as an example of the practice in the Baltic Sea region.

In the present situation of multiple carrier liability regimes, the shipping industry would greatly benefit from a single set of rules that balances shippers' and carriers' interests. The proposed United Nations Commission on International Trade Law's (UNCITRAL) Rules might be the answer to that problem. If the UNCITRAL Rules prove to be widely attractive for shippers and carriers alike, they could solve three types of problems. First of all, the general use of one set of rules would eliminate unforeseeability stemming from law of forum selecting when solving disputes. Second, the UNCITRAL Rules aim to revise and perfect the existing International Rules governing carriage of goods by sea. Third, the Rules incorporate provisions previously unregulated regarding modern developments in shipping.

No area is unaffected by factors surrounding it, and certainly carriage of goods by sea is affected by other modes of carriage (by road, rail and air). My area of research, although touching upon intermodal carriage, is limited to carriage of goods by sea.

In this thesis I take a closer look at carriage of goods by sea under a bill of lading. This arrangement has been by far the most popular way of transporting goods by sea in the whole world. In the first part of my thesis I will cover the international conventions governing shipping under a bill of a lading. As general background information I will explain the different functions and the procedure of issuing a bill of lading. In order to create a wholesome picture of the situation, it is essential that I also give a brief account of the history and development of carrier liability under different rules regulating carriage of goods by sea under a bill of lading. This will also describe the power struggle between the shipper and the carrier. By looking at the deal breakers of the past we will know what we are dealing with. However, to create successful (meaning highly popular) Rules, the interests of shippers and carriers must be balanced so that both parties will find them appealing.

Each of the international conventions was an answer to a problem in the shipping industry and represented the changed circumstances. The first international convention incorporating Hague Rules limited the wide discretion of carrier liability. Then amendments were made to it – which are known as the Hague-Visby Rules – to further specify and increase carrier's liabilities. The following convention incorporating the Hamburg Rules differed from previous ones as much more shipper-oriented. Unlike Hague and Hague-Visby Rules, the Hamburg Rules were not drafted by an association of old maritime nations, but by the United Nations under the initiative of cargo owning States. The circumstances have changed the most after drafting of the Hamburg Rules. Development of containerisation and technology used in shipping, have made it possible. Computer technology, which has had a tremendous impact on shipping industry, has evolved a great deal since adoption of the Hamburg Rules in 1978. Tendencies in global commerce have created a need for transporting goods over distances using different modes of carriage. The work on a uniform set of rules governing multimodal transport by United Nations Commission on International Trade Law is currently in progress. With States using different rules to cover maritime trade, international shipping is often full of surprises and differences. Uniform rules would contribute to foreseeability and lower costs. However, the new set of rules are surrounded by controversy as the previous United Nations Convention did not receive much support from shipowning nations, which in turn means exclusion of the vast majority of world's tonnage. I will describe the modern developments and analyze the UNCITRAL Draft Instrument in greater detail in the second part of my thesis.

In the third part of my thesis I will take Estonia as an example of a state applying its national law governing carriage of goods by sea under a bill of lading. This is an example of a state in the Baltic Sea region, influenced by legislative environments of its neighbors and the politics concerning transport. As Estonia is a Member State of European Union I will also touch upon the European Union legislation regarding shipping. Finally, I will look through the example of Estonia, what the practical advantage of the UNCITRAL Rules might be.

Although I start off with attention turned to bills of lading, the developments in the industry, as well as the practice in Baltic Sea region prove that in this particular location, right now, the bill does not really have the predicted supremacy. Neither does the UNCITRAL Instrument use the term 'bill of lading'.

It is only fair that I thoroughly acquaint myself and the reader with the topic at hand first, because only with sufficient information available, it is possible to draw any conclusions. In order to create a wholesome picture and explain the background regarding the subject matter at hand, large parts of this thesis are descriptive. In this thesis I am using historic approach while giving a brief account of the history and development of carrier liability under different rules regulating carriage of goods by sea under a bill of lading. International Rules governing carrier liability have evolved from the *ius cogens* described in the history and development section. All of the Rules are interwoven and have more similarities between them than differences. In my work I am focusing on the differences, because it is important to acknowledge the differences in order to obtain an adequate picture of the situation. To ascertain the differences and similarities I also compare the International Conventions on carrier liability and use comparative and normative approach.

In my work I describe, compare and criticize instruments that are recent (with the exception of Hague Rules) and not even completed yet (the UNCITRAL Instrument). This makes it rather difficult to gather the material. Largely it is gathered from web sites of institutions concerned with these instruments. 'Youth' of the instruments is also the reason why there is not much case law available. With minimum amount of case law and information about practice of the instruments available, I am clearly discussing the theory side of carriage of goods by sea. And what concerns the UNCITRAL Instrument, it must be kept in mind that it is still in the process of being drafted, and subject to further changes. Even so, it is possible to predict its success to an extent. In fact, it is even better to dissect a draft that provides several ways of solving problems.

B   Essence of the bill of lading and the problem with multiple rules governing carriage of goods by sea

I   Definition of the Bill of lading

A bill of lading is a document employed in the course of carriage of goods by sea. It need not be used in every type of carriage of goods by sea. In the case where the whole ship is at the dispense of one shipper, no bill of lading is necessary. However, if the shipper does not need the carrying capacity of the whole ship to transport his goods, he is likely to reserve some space on a liner that regularly sails an advertised route, or a tramp vessel that travels from one port to another in search of cargo. Once the shipper has opted for either of the last two possibilities, he may demand to be issued a bill of lading. The bill of lading allows transfer of ownership of goods while still in transit, thereby making trading faster.

II   History and development of the Bill of lading

The bill of lading has gone through an evolution lasting several centuries, thereby influencing the trade of carriage of goods by sea immensely. The bill of lading of fourteenth century[1] was just a receipt issued by a shipowner against the cargo received to a merchant who didn't wish to travel with his goods. Such bill stated the type and quantity of goods and the condition in which they were received. This information was later incorporated into the terms of contract of carriage. By eighteenth century the bill of lading had become negotiable by indorsement so that goods could be sold while in transit.[2] The merchants regarded the bill of lading along with Certificate of Insurance[3] as the cargo, which it represents.[4]

Before the nineteenth century, the common law required carriers to exercise "the near absolute duty to 'insure' the safety of the goods against all but *force majeure*[5] and act of the Queen's

---

[1] Some authorities indicate that bills of lading might have been widely in use already in the thirteenth century. See http://www.fordham.edu/halsall/source/1248billoflading.html. "Medieval Sourcebook: Bill of Lading, 1248". Website last accessed 22 Oct 2004.

[2] John F. Wilson, "Carriage of Goods by sea", 2001, 4th edition, Pearson Education Limited, at p 119.

[3] A 'fob' (free on board) contract would give seller a certificate of insurance, whereas a 'cif' (cost insurance freight) contract gives seller a bill of lading. Robert Grime, "Shipping Law", 1991, 2nd edition, London, Sweet & Maxwell, at p 157, 158.

[4] Grime, at p 122.

[5] Italics hereinforth inserted by the author of this Thesis.

enemies"[6]. But when the concept of freedom of contract began to develop in the nineteenth century, the carriers were able to take advantage of their position and exclude their common law liabilities to a rather large extent. As a result, model bills of lading were drawn up to restrict shipowners' in limiting their liability.[7]

This lead up to the drafting of a set of rules by the Maritime Law Committee of the International Law Association. These rules came to be known as Hague Rules. After negotiations and amendments they became incorporated in an international convention in 1924. This convention intended to unify specific rules relating to bills of lading and to ensure certain standards, securing some protection for the cargo owner.[8] Nearly half a century later, in February 1968, the Hague Rules were amended by the Brussels Protocol[9], affording cargo owners a wider scale of protection.[10] Just ten years later United Nations Convention on the Carriage of Goods by Sea (Hamburg Rules) was signed.[11] With so many options for different degrees of limitation of carrier's liability available, there is a division in states applying a certain set of rules: many shipowning states are still loyal to the original Hague Rules, 29 have adopted the Hague-Visby amendments, 26 (mostly African) states have adopted the Hamburg Rules, and a fourth group[12] has a hybrid system comprised of Hague-Visby and Hamburg regimes.[13]

III Functions of a bill of lading

Four[14] distinct functions can be identified in a bill of lading – it is a receipt for goods shipped; an evidence of the contract of carriage; a document transferring constructive possession; and a document of title.

---

[6] Grime at p 125.
[7] Wilson at p 119-20.
[8] Wilson at p 120.
[9] "The revised rules incorporating the amendments contained in the Brussels Protocol are known as the 'Hague/Visby Rules'." Wilson at p 121.
[10] Wilson at p 120-121.
[11] This convention only entered into force on 1 November 1992. Wilson at p 121.
[12] Including Australia, for example. See further discussion below on page 25!
[13] Wilson at p 121.
[14] Many of my sources (August at p 612, Black's Law dictionary, Grime at p 125, Schoenbaum at 507) cite three functions, omitting the function as a document transferring constructive possession. Wilson mentions this function as a subtopic when talking about bill of lading's function as a document of title, differentiating the two by the factor of intent to transfer the ownership in goods. However, Richard Caddell, in his Carriage of Goods by Sea lecture of fall 2003 in International University Concordia Audentes, mentions four functions of a bill of lading. I think this approach is justified because a bill of

10

First, a function what the bill of lading started to evolve from – **function as a receipt for goods shipped**[15]. It is in the interest of both the carrier and the shipper that statements about quantity and quality of goods are marked down on the bill of lading.[16] The shipper would want information about the goods marked down as accurately as possible in case the goods turn out to be damaged or short on discharge, as that would be the basis of a cargo claim.[17] The carrier, on the other hand, should inspect the goods and note down any obvious defects (that packages are not damaged and that labels comply)[18]. A bill of lading with such a mark is a "claused bill".[19] However, a "clean bill of lading"[20] would be much more desirable for the shipper as banks require it in order to qualify for a credit, or it might make it difficult to sell the goods.[21] If the carrier has no means of inspecting the goods, as the case may be with containers, he shall mark down on the bill of lading "said to contain". Such a phrase is capable of reducing the liability of the carrier.[22]

Second, a bill of lading is an **evidence of a contract of carriage**. A bill of lading is not necessarily the contract of carriage itself even though the reverse side[23] of a standard liner bill of lading form states "a detailed set of printed contractual terms or a reference to the 'long form' bill in which they are set out in full"[24], "but [it] is usually the best evidence of the contract"[25]. The contract is considered to be the oral[26] agreement that is made long before the bill is issued (and the carrier's advertisements, the booking note, the freight tariff and practices known and accepted

---

lading's function as a document transferring constructive possession presents possibilities that are clearly different from the other functions, therefore I have decided to divide it into a function of its own. Source personally made class notes.
[15] Bold hereinforth inserted by the author of this Thesis.
[16] A bill of lading may also include leading (or identifying) marks, date of issuing the bill. Wilson at p 132-134.
[17] Wilson at p 122.
[18] Ray August, "International Business Law", 3rd edition, 2000, Prentice –Hall at p 611.
[19] Grime at p 150.
[20] Also known in the United States as "on board bill of lading". August at p 612.
[21] August at p 612, Grime at p 150 & Wilson at p 128, 131.
[22] Grime at p 150 & Wilson at p 132.
[23] See the first page of the Appendix for the reverse side of liner bill of lading used by TECO Lines!
[24] Wilson at p 3.
[25] Tetley, "Chapter 1, Application of the Rules generally". Available at
<http://upload.mcgill.ca/maritimelaw/ch1marine.pdf> Website last accessed 1 March 2005.
[26] On certain circumstances oral agreements can be binding in common law states. In civil law states the contract usually comprises of earlier agreements, exchange of emails, faxes. In the Ardennes case the court looked at oral agreements as the contract rather than the terms on back of the bill of lading.

by the shipper)[27]. [28] The shipper or the carrier may produce evidence of terms not stated in the bill of lading when a dispute arises. However, no other evidence may be introduced once the bill is negotiated to a bona fide third party. The reason this is so is because the endorsee can only be aware of the terms of carriage stated in the bill of lading.[29] Another consequence of the bill being an evidence of a contract of carriage is that the shipper still has remedy if the goods are lost or damaged before a bill is issued (or if the printed terms on the bill do not comply with earlier agreements).[30]

In the case when a voyage charterer agrees to carry cargo other than its own, a bill of lading may be issued, but the carriage is still ruled by the provisions of the charterparty. Then, the bill of lading is not considered an evidence of contract of carriage, but merely as a receipt for goods shipped. Once again, when the bill is endorsed, the holder of the bill of lading is to presume that the contract of carriage is restricted to the terms stated in the bill.[31]

The third function of a bill of lading – as a document **transferring constructive possession** – allows transfer of the right of possession of goods without transferring the right of ownership. This function differs from the bill of lading's function as evidence of title since there is no intent to transfer the ownership in the goods present. Such function proves useful when a seller of goods wants to keep "ownership as security for payment of the price" or when goods are moved between two branches of a multinational corporation. The possession of goods may also be transferred in order to temporarily secure a loan.[32]

There are two kinds of bills of lading – 'order' bills and 'straight' bills. The latter means that the goods covered by it are to be delivered to a named consignee only, which makes the bill non-negotiable. Such bills are also called waybills.[33] 'Order' or ordinary bills of lading, however, function as **evidence of title** as well. This means that by transferring the bill, the goods can be

---

[27] Tetley, "Chapter 1, Application of the Rules generally".
[28] Wilson at p 134-135.
[29] August, at 616, Wilson at p 135.
[30] Wilson at p 134.
[31] Wilson at p 135, 137 & Grime at 151.
[32] Wilson at p 140.
[33] Wilson at p 137 & August at p 616.

sold while still in transit or used to raise credit with the bank.[34] The holder of the 'order' bill is entitled to delivery of the goods by surrendering the bill. These characteristics make the bill of lading quite flexible and therefore popular. In order to engage goods that are at sea in a contract of sale, a bill of lading and its ability to function as an evidence of title is essential. There may be a number of reasons why the seller would want to dispose of the goods while they are still in transit – to save time, to save money. As an evidence of title, the bill of lading can be used to raise credit with bank. The constructive possession is transferred to the bank until the goods have been paid for. Moreover, the holder of the bill of lading has the title to sue the carrier under the contract of carriage, when he otherwise would not have that right in common law, since he is considered a third party. But the courts have agreed to "imply a contract between consignee or indorsee and the carrier".[35]

IV Procedure of issuing a bill of lading

The individual with goods to ship contacts a shipping line (usually through an agent) and reserves some space on a vessel. The carrier then informs that individual of the time and place to deliver the goods. When the goods are handed over, the owner of goods is issued with a receipt stating type and quantity of the goods and the condition in which they were received by the carrier's agent. The carrier then takes care of loading the goods aboard. At the same time the shipper acquires a copy of carrier's bill of lading form and enters details about the shipment, including the name of the consignee. Carrier's agent checks whether the details filled in by the shipper correspond to cargo details at the time of loading. If the statements are correct, he will acknowledge them if so is requested. Freight is then calculated and entered on the bill, which is signed by the master or his agent and released to the shipper. The shipper may send the bill to the consignee or to a bank.[36] Either way, the consignee is free to sell the cargo while in transit and indorse the bill in favour of the purchaser. The cargo is released at the port of discharge to whoever (the ultimate consignee or indorsee of the bill) produces the bill of lading.[37] Handing

---

[34] Wilson at p 137.
[35] Wilson at p 141-142.
[36] If a letter of credit is involved, the seller's bank forwards the letter of credit to the buyer's bank. Thomas J. Schoenbaum, "Admiralty and Maritime Law", 1994, 2nd edition, West Publishing Co. See pages 467-470.
[37] Wilson at p 121-122, August at p 612.

over the cargo to whoever produces the original bill of lading is the key element of how the bill of lading works.[38]

V International rules

> "A study of the historical events which brought the Hague and Hague/Visby Rules about is not only advisable, but at times necessary, in order to understand how one law was built on another or how it answered a particular need of commerce."[39]

I would like to go even further in my study and include Hamburg Rules in my brief overview as the UNCITRAL D.I. borrows many of the ideas and approaches from Hamburg Rules as well.

There are currently three sets of international rules that could be incorporated into a bill of lading: Hague Rules, Hague-Visby Rules and Hamburg Rules. I will now take a closer look at these Rules, explain briefly why they came about and what changes they brought along to international shipping. I will proceed in a chronological order, starting from the oldest, Hague Rules. The general principles that I have described already (functions of a bill of lading and the procedure of issuing a bill of lading) are considered to be included in the Hague Rules, therefore I will not repeat them. Neither will I mention the aspects that are similar to previous rules, but rather the differences. I will also leave out the aspects irrelevant from the point of view of this thesis.

a) The Hague Rules

International Convention for the Unification of Certain Rules of Law relating to Bills of Lading, also known as the Hague Rules, was signed in Brussels in 1924 and entered into force in 1931. It was based on a draft adopted by the International Law Association in the Hague in 1921, and amended at a diplomatic conference in Brussels in 1922 and in 1923.[40] "The Hague Rules were a compromise between carrier and shipper interests, designed to secure greater fairness as well as

---

[38] In practice, the whole procedure may not be that formal, and not always closely followed. When the shipper and carrier are not doing business for the first time, they trust each other, and a business practice has formed, they are just likely to email each other the minimal information necessary for the transaction. Afanasjev, Maxim, sales coordination manager of TECO LINES AS. Personal interview on the practices employed by TECO Lines AS regarding procedure of obtaining a bill of lading and other issues on 5 November 2004.

[39] William Tetley, Q.C., "Interpretation and Construction of the Hague, Hague/Visby and Hamburg Rules" (published in 2004) 10 JIML 30-70) <http://tetley.law.mcgill.ca/maritime/rulesinterpretation.pdf> Website last accessed 1 October 2004.

[40] Also known as the Brussels Convention. Tetley, "Chapter 1, Application of the Rules generally".

more uniform carriage of goods by sea law."[41] The Convention defines areas and limits of liabilities for the carrier, which may not be excluded and lowered even by mutual agreement[42], thereby providing some kind of basic protection of shippers' rights. This set forth the carrier's liability for negligence in the "loading, handling, stowage, carriage, custody, care and discharge"[43] of the goods, and providing a seaworthy[44] vessel. On the other hand, carrier was relieved from liability for absolute warranty of seaworthiness[45] and negligence in "navigation or in the management"[46] of the ship. Article 4 goes on to identify fifteen more exceptions when carrier is excluded from liability, and a clause stating "[a]ny other cause arising without the actual fault or privity of the carrier..."[47] Neither is deviation considered an infringement of the Convention or the contract of carriage while "saving or attempting to save life or property at sea, or any reasonable deviation".[48]

In case the nature and value of goods that are being transported exceeds 100 pounds sterling per package or unit, the shipper must make a note (constituting a prima facie evidence) of it in the bill of lading, otherwise the carrier will only be liable for loss or damage to the goods up to the aforementioned amount.[49] As one can see, although the Hague Rules attempted to balance the rights of shippers and carriers alike and "reign in the unbridled freedom of contract of owners"[50], the outcome was remarkably in favour of the carrier.[51] The Convention also tried to make the **outcome of litigation** in the courts of the contracting states the same. This attempt, however,

---

[41] Tetley, "Interpretation and Construction of the Hague, Hague/Visby and Hamburg Rules". at p 47
[42] "Any clause, covenant, or agreement in a contract of carriage relieving the carrier or the ship from liability for loss or damage to [...] goods [...] shall be null and void." The Hague Rules, Article 3(8). But the Rules permit greater liability and fewer rights for the carrier by agreement, if such agreement is then stated in the bill of lading. Article 5.
[43] The Hague Rules. Article 2.
[44] This is often understood to include cargoworthyness, although in the Hague Rules, cargoworthiness in referred to separately. Article 1 (a) and (c).
[45] However, the carrier was to excercise due diligence and bear the burden of proving that due diligence had been exercised if he wanted to claim that exemption. The Hague Rules. Article 4.
[46] The Hague Rules. Article 4(2)(a).
[47] The Hague Rules, Article 4(2)(q).
[48] The Hague Rules, Article 4(4).
[49] However, by agreement, it is possible to fix a higher maximum amount. The Hague Rules. Article 4(5).
[50] Lord Steyn, in Effort shipping Co. Ltd. V Linden Management S.A. [1998] 1 Lloyd's Rep. 337 at p. 346, 1998 AMC 1050 at p. 1065 (H.L.) Tetley, "Interpretation and Construction of the Hague, Hague/Visby and Hamburg Rules" at p 48.
[51] This was probably because of the better bargaining position of the shipowners (the carriers) due to the market situation and the interest and participation of the shipowning nations.

failed because of the different ways the Hague Rules were brought into force in signatory states. The Convention could be:

1. legally binding in the state without any national modifications;
2. enacted as a statute;
3. incorporated in national legislation[52]

This did not eliminate conflicts in determining the carriers' liability and the validity of negligence clauses in bills of lading, since states adopted the rules with modifications and textual variations, which accounted for formation of different rules and interpretations.[53]

Under the Hague Rules, suit against the carrier and the ship may be brought "within one year after delivery of the goods or the date when the goods should have been delivered", otherwise the liability in respect of loss or damage to goods shall be discharged.[54]

Extent of application of the Hague Rules

Hague Rules apply to "all contracts of carriage of goods by sea covered by a bill or a similar document of title" (including a waybill) unless the shipment is an extraordinary shipment in non-commercial trade issued in any of the contracting states[55]. Neither do the Hague Rules apply to the national coasting trade when so is stated by statute, or when deck cargo (which by contract of carriage is to be placed on deck) or live animals are involved.[56] It is irrelevant whether the bill of lading is actually issued.[57] A contract is considered to be 'covered' by a bill of lading when a bill of lading is intended to be issued.[58] The Hague Rules can be made to apply to charterparties by a proper and logical express statement,[59] otherwise the application would be dismissed as Article 5 of the Convention states that charter parties are excluded. Bills of ladings issued under a charter party are, however, covered by the Hague Rules.[60] If a bill of lading is issued but the carrier does not receive the goods, the contract of carriage has not commenced and the Hague rules do not apply.[61]

---

[52] Falkanger at p 261.
[53] Schoenbaum at p 524.
[54] The Hague Rules. Article 3.6.
[55] The Hague Rules. Articles 6 & 10.
[56] See Hague Rules, Article 1 (c).
[57] Tetley, "Chapter 1, Application of the Rules generally".
[58] Pyrene Co. V. Scindia Steam Navigaton Co., Ltd [1954] 2 QB 402 at pp 419-420, [1954] 1 Lloyd's Rep. 321 at p 329.
[59] Tetley, "Chapter 1, Application of the Rules generally" at p 16.
[60] Tetley, "Chapter 1, Application of the Rules generally" at p 17.
[61] Tetley, "Chapter 1, Application of the Rules generally" at p 16.

The Hague Rules are not necessarily meant to apply to the whole contract of carriage (in case of an intermodal contract of carriage) – Article 1(e) specifies 'carriage of goods' to mean "from the time when the goods are loaded on to the time they are discharged from the ship". This is understood as covering the 'tackle to tackle'[62] period when the carrier is responsible for loading and discharge.

b) The Hague-Visby Rules

The Hague Rules proved to be in need of a reform. The amending Visby Rules were the result of the Comité Maritime International (CMI) Conference in 1963, which were formally adopted as the "Protocol to Amend the International Convention for the Unification of Certain Rules of Law Relating to Bills of Lading" by a diplomatic conference in Brussels in 1968[63]. The amended version came to be known as the Hague-Visby Rules.

The Visby Rules updated the carrier/shipper **liability** slightly more in favour of shippers.[64] Rule IV Article 5 was initially amended to increase the amount the carrier would be liable for to "10 000 francs per package or unit or 30 francs per kilo of gross weight of the goods lost or damaged, whichever is the higher".[65] A protocol that was concluded eleven years later replaced the amount with "666.67 units of account per package or unit or 2 units of account per kilo of gross weight of the goods lost or damage, whichever is the higher".[66] The unit of account that was referred to was the Special Drawing Right (SDR) used by International Monetary Fund. Its value is based on "basket" of key currencies and is published daily. Since the value of SDR fluctuates daily, and because of the different ways of converting into national currencies, many countries that apply Hague or Hague-Visby Rules, have adopted a "gold clause agreement",

---

[62] "From the time when the ship's tackle is hooked onto the cargo at the port of loading until the hook of the tackle is released at the port of discharge. Where the shore tackle is used, the operative period will normally be from the time the cargo crosses the ship's rail during loading until it recrosses the rail during discharge." Wilson at 184.
[63] The Protocol entered into force June 23, 1977.
[64] Tetley, "Interpretation and Construction of the Hague, Hague/Visby and Hamburg Rules" at p 48.
[65] The Protocol to Amend the International Convention for the Unification of Certain Rules of Law Relating to Bills of Lading ("Visby Rules"), Article 2 (a).
[66] Protocol (also known as the SDR Prototcol) amending the International Convention for the Unification of Certain Rules of Law relating to Bills of Lading of 25 August 1924, as amended by the Protocol of 23 February 1968, Article II (1)(a). This protocol entered into force in 1984.

which fixes the package limitation formula to a specific amount of their own currency. Therefore, even states that apply the same rules, have different limitations.[67]

Article IV Rule 5 (e) forbids the carrier's right to limit its liability if proved that the damage "resulted from an act or omission of the carrier done with intent to cause damage, or recklessly and with knowledge that damage would probably result".

Extent of application of the Hague-Visby Rules

The Visby Rules amend the Hague Rules by extending their scope of application. Not only do they apply to "bills of lading issued in any of the contracting states", but also to carriage "from a port in a Contracting State" and to contracts that provide "that the rules of this Convention or legislation of any State giving effect to them are to govern the contract".[68]

Thereby making irrelevant the nationality of the ship, the carrier, the shipper, the consignee, or any other interested person.

c) Hamburg Rules

The Brussels Protocol of 1968, amending the Hague Rules (the Visby Rules) were not seen by the cargo owning nations as the solution to the situation regulating carrier liability, but rather as a temporary fix. The Hague-Visby Rules did not adequately cover many aspects of carriage of goods by sea, and they represented the interests of traditional maritime nations, rather than the whole industry. Comprehensive initiative to revise the Hague and Hague-Visby Rules was undertaken by the UN agencies UNCTAD[69] and UNCITRAL[70]. A convention based on an UNCITRAL draft succeeding the Hague Rules was adopted in March 1978 at a diplomatic conference in Hamburg. The Convention, known as the 'Hamburg Rules'[71], entered into force on 1 November 1992.

---

[67] Schoenbaum at p 525.
[68] The Visby Rules, Article 5.
[69] United Nations Conference on Trade and Development
[70] United Nations Commission on International Trade Law
[71] United Nationas Convention on the Carriage of Goods by Sea ("The Hamburg Rules), signed at Hamburg on March 31, 1978.

28 states[72] (mostly developing countries and landlocked states, constituting roughly 5% of world maritime trade)[73] have adopted the Hamburg Rules, but none of the major maritime states, because it changes the way carrier's liability is looked at. It has a major impact on cargo insurance rates and practice.[74] First of all, the Hamburg Rules clearly prefer the interests of cargo owners as the concept of carrier liability is completely reversed in the sense that the burden to prove his innocence lies on the carrier. This idea is evidenced in the wording of Article 5 (1):

> *"The carrier is liable* for loss resulting from loss of or damage to the goods, as well as delay in delivery, if the occurrence which caused the loss, damage or delay took place while the goods were in his charge as defined in article 4, *unless the carrier proves* that he, his servants or agents took all measures that could reasonably be required to avoid the occurrence and its consequences."

Carrier liability is based on fault. The catalogue of exceptions provided by Hague and the Hague-Visby Rules is abolished.[75] A rather significant change in carrier liability is evidenced in abolition of the exception captured in Article IV rule 2(a) of the Hague-Visby Rules covering the exclusion of liability for "act, neglect, or default of the master, mariner, pilot, or the servants of the carrier in the navigation or in the management of the ship". This exception was the traditional maritime protection that does not extend to carriers in any other mode of transport. Said provision along with carrier's duty of care to cargo had been the source of uncertainty and litigation. By placing the burden of proof on the carrier in all cases reduces the confusion. Moreover, the carrier is usually better placed to have more knowledge of facts and causes. [76]

The Hamburg Rules have a slightly different approach to carriage of **live animals** and **deck cargo** as the Hague or Hague-Visby Rules do. Shipping of **'particular goods'** is not excluded from coverage of the Rules, but they are governed by special provisions.[77] Carriage of live animals is dealt with in Article 5(5), which limits carrier's liability in case of "loss, damage or

---

[72] Status of ratifications of Maritime Conventions. United Nations Convention on the Carriage of Goods by sea. Hamburg, 31 March 1978. Available at
<http://www.comitemaritime.org/ratific/uninat/uni02.html> Website last accessed 1 February 2005.
[73] UN Hamburg Rules of 1978. Available at
<http://www.oecd.org/document/13/0,2340,en_2649_34337_1866253_119666_1_1_1,00.html> Web page last accessed 1 February 2005.
[74] August at p 611. Wilson at p 213. Falkanger at p 262. Schoenbaum at p 525.
[75] Article IV rule 2(c)-(p) & Wilson at p 214.
[76] Wilson at p 215-216.
[77] Wilson at p 216-217.

delay in delivery resulting from any special risks inherent in that kind of carriage" unless there is proof that carrier has not "complied with any special instructions given" by the shipper. Article 9 governs the carriage of deck cargo. As is the case in Hague and Hague-Visby Rules, "the carrier is entitled to carry the goods on deck only if such carriage is in accordance with an agreement with the shipper or with usage of the particular trade or is required by statutory rules of regulations"[78]. The carrier is obliged to insert in the bill of lading[79] a statement to that effect. Yet, unlike Hague and Hague-Visby Rules, the Hamburg Rules do apply to carriage of deck cargo.

The Hague nor the Hague-Visby Rules regulate the recovery of loss caused by late delivery (**delay**) of cargo. These rules impose just the obligation of careful handling of the goods, but no recovery for economic loss (loss of market) caused by delay in delivery. The Hamburg Rules aim to bring carriage of goods by sea "in line with carriage by three other modes of international transport", meaning carriage by air, road and rail, all of which have provisions dealing with loss resulting from delay in delivery. The standard burden of proof could still be applied there – carrier can escape liability by proving neither he, his servants, or agents were at fault.[80]

Although there were sentiments to the contrary of preserving the principle of **limitation of liability** at the time of drafting the Hamburg Rules, they still remained, as they allowed the carrier to make predictions and calculate cheaper freight rates. On the other hand, the limits needed to be quite high to make sure the carrier is interested in looking after the goods properly. The limit of liability is 25 per cent higher than in Hague-Visby Rules. The Hamburg Rules have SDR as their unit of account, just like the Protocol Amending Hague-Visby Rules introduced. In Hamburg Rules the liability of the carrier is "limited to an amount equivalent to 835 units of account per package or other shipping unit or 2.5 units of account per kilogram of gross weight of the goods lost or damaged, whichever is the higher".[81] These limits apply to loss or damage to the goods. The liability for delay is dealt with in Article 6.1(b).[82]

---

[78] The Hamburg Rules. Article 9.1.
[79] ..or other document evidencing the contract of carriage by sea.. The Hamburg Rules. Article 9.2.
[80] Wilson at p 218-219.
[81] The Hague. Article 6.1(a).
[82] Wilson at p 219-220.

Limitation of actions under Hamburg Rules is extended to two years[83] instead of one under Hague and Hague-Visby Rules.[84] One more difference lies in the fact that the Hague and Hague-Visby Rules do not mention the possibility of limiting actions against shipper.

Unlike Hague and Hague-Visby Rules, the Hamburg Rules include provisions governing forum selection (**jurisdiction**). Judicial or arbitral proceedings relating to carriage of goods under the Hamburg Rules may be brought in defendant's principal place of business,[85] in the place of the contract was made,[86] in the port of loading or discharge or at any other place stated for that purpose in the contract.[87] The judicial proceedings may also be instigated "in the courts of any port or place in a Contracting State at which the carrying vessel or any other vessel of the same ownership may have been arrested". In such case the defendant has the right to demand removal of the action to one of the above-mentioned jurisdictions. However, the defendant "must furnish security sufficient to ensure payment of any judgment" against him.[88]

Extent of application of Hamburg Rules

The Hamburg Rules, compared to Hague and Hague-Visby Rules, have by far the widest scope of application. They apply if the port of loading or discharge[89] is located in a Contracting State, or if "one of the optional ports of discharge provided for in the contract of carriage by sea is the actual port of discharge and such port is located in a Contracting State". The Hamburg Rules also apply if "the bill of lading or other document evidencing the contract of carriage by sea is issued in a Contracting State", or if such document "provides that the provisions of this Convention or the legislation of any State giving effect to them are to govern the contract".[90] Neither is it important for the purpose of application of Hamburg rules "whether a bill of lading or a non-negotiable receipt is issued".[91]

---

[83] The Hamburg Rules. Article 20.1.
[84] See page 18!
[85] ...or in case there is none – in the habitual residence of the defendant.
[86] ...if the defendant has a place of business, branch or agency there, through which the contract was made.
[87] The Hamburg Rules. Articles 21.1 & 22.3.
[88] The Hamburg Rules. Article 21.2.
[89] The Hamburg Rules governing both inward and outward bills is a very important factor as doing business with states that apply the Hamburg Rules is affected by that.
[90] The Hamburg Rules. Article 2 (1).
[91] Wilson at 213, Hamburg Rules, Article 1.7.

The period of responsibility of the carrier under Hamburg Rules is longer than under Hague and Hague-Visby Rules where the tackle-to-tackle principle is applied. The Hamburg Rules may be considered to apply a port-to-port rule. Under Hamburg Rules the carrier is in charge of the goods already at the port of loading, which may well mean while the goods are still in a warehouse, since the time commences from the moment carrier has taken over the goods. The carrier remains responsible for the goods until he has handed them to the consignee[92] or an authority or other third party assigned by law or regulations applicable at the port of discharge.[93]

d) Criticism of the Hague, Hague-Visby and the Hamburg Rules

Neither the Hague nor the Hague-Visby Rules are without faults. The Hamburg Rules have even managed to eliminate some of their faults. However, it is almost impossible to make a concise criticism of Hague and Hague-Visby Rules. These Rules are mainly the result of a natural process incorporating efficient practice that has been exercised by major shipping nations over the centuries. Yet, the greatest fault with the Hague an Hague-Visby Rules seems to be that they are not liked by cargo owning states as the balance of interest leans towards shipowners. The Hamburg Rules are rules designed for cargo owners. This in itself would not pose a problem, however, the Rules are the result of diplomatic compromises which has made the language of the Rules vague, but most of all – they are not based on extensive practice.

When it comes to the Hamburg Rules, cargo owners are clearly supporters, and the shipowners are opposed to these Rules. Cargo owners favor the Rules since they abolish the catalogue of exceptions, and delete the exclusion of liability for negligent navigation. Higher liability interests are also to shippers' liking as the carrier might be more interested in taking better care of the goods. Shipowners are opposed to the Rules losing the catalogue of exceptions, including the traditional exclusion of liability for negligent navigation. They are against the doubling of the limitation period, and higher liability limits. This is simply inevitable because of directly opposite interests of the parties. However, both parties would have to admit that the Hamburg Rules have made some bold adjustments - placing the burden of proof on carrier as the party who has access

---

[92] ...or placed them at the disposal of the consignee in accordance with the contract, law or usage of the particular trade applicable at the port of discharge. Article 4.2(b)(ii). Tetley finds that „the carrier may contract out of responsibility after tackle by a general clause in the bill of lading or may try to invoke custom". Tetley, "Chapter1, Application of the Rules generally".

[93] The Hamburg Rules. Article 4.

to the evidence, and eliminating the clause that permits exclusion of liability for negligent navigation (which essentially means no liability for one's own negligent actions). Hamburg Rules certainly try to move towards a uniform regime of carrier liability. Perhaps a little unfairly and thoughtlessly, the Rules are made to apply mandatorily not only to outgoing cargoes, but to incoming cargoes as well. This will cause uneasy situations when a cargo leaves from a state mandatorily applying Hague or Hague-Visby Rules and reaches a port in a state applying the Hamburg Rules. The decision of which rules are applicable would not be clear until a forum is selected. Due to the wide choice, the final forum would not be easy to predict. Then it is up to the forum to apply its local law in deciding which Rules to apply.[94]

e) Hybrid regimes and the problem of plurality of Rules

The current situation with states adhering to different rules regulating carrier liability under bills of lading creates a mosaic picture. Not only are the differences created by the essence of three different Rules, but the states themselves are also creating variations of these rules by adopting some ideas from one set of rules and others from another set of rules. Such states are known as applying hybrid regimes. Major maritime nations applying hybrid regimes are: China, Japan, Scandinavian states[95] and Australia.[96] According to Wilson, states should "refrain from devising their own national or regional solution to the problem" as this makes international uniformity even harder to achieve.[97]

Points to be noted when dealing with, for example, the Australian rules are the kind of documents that are governed by the rules, whether the rules also cover deck cargo (and under which circumstances), the period of carrier's liability, conditions for carrier's liability for delay and the conditions for Australian arbitration to apply. Moreover, one certainly needs to know that the

---

[94] Wilson at p 225-227.
[95] According to Falkanger "the rules in Norwegian Maritime Code have been aligned with the Hamburg Rules as far as possible without having to derrogate from the Hague-Visby Convention." At p 264. Since the Estonian legislation combines Hague-Visby and Hamburg Rules, while following Scandinavian laws, Estonia can be included in that list of countries applying hybrid regimes.
[96] Wilson at p 227.
[97] Wilson at p 228.

Australian rules will apply, if incoming carriage is not governed by Hague, Hague-Visby, or the Hamburg Rules (or a substantially similar regime).[98]

VI Conclusion

Simply due to the fact that there are currently three sets of international Rules and several more rules made up of fragments of these international Rules (the hybrid regimes), creates some significant problems to carriers, operators and shippers across the globe. The major problem is the unforeseeability as to which Rules apply.

> "Currently large sums of money, 'which would be better applied commercially, are spent in legal disputes as to whether the contract terms or a Convention and, if so which Convention, should apply to govern relations between contracting parties'."[99]

The shipping industry would greatly benefit from adopting a single set of rules, which combine the most efficient aspects of the different rules.

---

[98] Ian Davis, "COGSA 98: The Australian Carriage of Goods by Sea Act". International Maritime Law, 1998, 7.

[99] Malcolm Clarke, "A conflict of conventions: The UNCITRAL/CMI draft transport instrument on your doorstep". Journal of International Maritime Law, 2003, no 1, p 28. quote in quote: Faber, 'The problems arising out of multimodal transport' [1996] L.M.C.L.Q. 503 to 518, at 518. & Alcantara [2002] L.M.C.L.Q. 399, 403 to 404.

C UNCITRAL Draft Instrument as the answer to the problem of plurality of Rules

The UNCITRAL Draft Instrument intends to gather together into a single international convention various items concerning carriage of goods by sea. It incorporates the subjects that international Rules traditionally include, including scope of application, issues of liability, limitation of liability and rights and obligations of the parties. However, the Draft Instrument is much more detailed than the previous Rules and provides explanations of several aspects that other international conventions on carrier liability do not touch upon. Moreover, it also includes provisions regulating modern developments in carriage of goods by sea.

I will first give a brief overview of the development process of the the UNCITRAL Draft Instrument. The development process deals with previously regulated and unregulated aspects together. Then I will discuss traditional areas of regulation (which include aspects that have previously remained unwritten yet in essence form the *ius cogens* of carriage of goods by sea)[100] separately from previously unregulated areas (here I mean areas created by technological developments).

The development process in itself is an argument in favor of the new Rules. Although it is an UNCITRAL Instrument, it was originally drafted by CMI which previously produced the Visby amendments to the Hague Rules. CMI of all the institutions should know the scope of this task, since the harmonization of maritime law has been its far-reaching ambition.[101] The involvement of national associations and international organizations is impressive as well. An overview of the development process might provide an idea how the future developments turn out since the instrument is still largely in the process of being completed.

---

[100] I will also provide comparisons with other International Rules when there are comparable provisions present.
[101] Comite Maritime International "A Brief Structural History of the First Century" Available at <http://www.comitemaritime.org/histo/his.html> Website last visited 1 February 2005.

I The development process of the UNICTRAL Draft Instrument as the right way forward

UNCITRAL expressed the need for a uniform set of rules in the areas where no such rules existed after its 29th Session in 1996:

> "existing national laws and international conventions left significant gaps regarding issues such as the functioning of the bill of lading and sea waybills, the relation of those transport documents to the rights and obligations between the seller and the buyer of goods, and to the legal position of the entities that provided financing to a party to the contract of carriage."

Unlike the Hamburg Rules, which artificially attempted to find solutions to unregulated problems and ignored experience gained from practice from shipping nations in an attempt to remedy injustice towards cargo owning nations, the UNCITRAL opted for a thorough research of present practices and actual needs.

UNCITRAL asked the CMI and other organizations "to gather information about current practices and laws in the area of international carriage of goods by sea".[102] CMI established an International Working Group on Issues of Transport Law in May 1998. The Working Group collaborated with sixteen National Maritime Law Associations in sorting out the principle issues for discussion. Issues of liability were included in the project in May 1999. After the UNCITRAL/CMI Colloquium the idea that liability regime be extended beyond the sea leg started to develop. Since 2001 at the Singapore Conference the facilitation of electronic commerce was to be included in the project.

The draft of the CMI Instrument was commented on by fifteen National Associations and nine international organizations. Individuals and organizations within and outside the CMI contributed to the CMI Draft Instrument. The CMI Draft Instrument on Transport Law was presented to the UNCITRAL on 11 December 2001.[103]

---

[102] Comite Maritime International's Draft Instrument on Carriage of Goods [wholly or partly] [by sea]. Available at <http://www.comitemaritime.org/draft/draft.html> Last accessed 1 February 2005.
[103] See CMI's Draft at <http://www.comitemaritime.org/draft/draft.html>!

UNITRAL established its Working Group III on Transport Law in 2001 at its 34th session.[104] It was to continue the work on the project. The title of the Draft Instrument upon presentation to the UNCITRAL was "Draft Instrument on Transport Law". It was changed to "Preliminary Draft Instrument on Carriage of Goods by Sea". Later the title was changed to "Draft Instrument on the Carriage of Goods [by Sea]". At the moment the title is "Draft Instrument on the Carriage of Goods [wholly or partly] [by Sea]".[105]

Paragraph 13 of the Introduction of the preliminary draft instrument on the carriage of goods by sea points out the gaps between mandatory regimes and proposes liability coverage for the full duration of carrier's custody of the cargo. Thereby extending the draft to govern multimodal transport.[106]

The definition of the carrier in the first version of UNCITRAL Draft Instrument is the same as under Hague-Visby Rules – a contractual person. As a new feature, the Draft provides a definition of the container, as well as electronic communication and electronic record, which intends to cover every type of system existing now and in future. Unlike the Hague and Hague-Visby Rules, reference to delay is made. What concerns carriage of goods on deck, provision addressing specially fitted containers is added.

Paragraph 30 explains why reference to a bill of lading is no more made. Although application of international conventions has been tied to a bill of lading before, the "bills of lading have been increasingly replaced by other, often non-negotiable, documents". It is also expected that traditional documents will become less relevant.[107] Moreover, such situation is also possible that in trades where negotiable documents are not common, the carrier is not obliged to issue a

---

[104] A/CN.9/WG.III/WP.32 - Transport Law: Draft instrument on the carriage of goods [wholly or partly] [by sea] - Note by the Secretariat. Twelfth session, Vienna, 6-17 October 2003. Available at: <http://www.uncitral.org/english/workinggroups/wg_3/WP32-FINAL.%20REVISION%203%20Sept.pdf> Web page last accessed 22 March 2005.
[105] See CMI's Draft.
[106] A/CN.9/WG.III/WP.21 - Transport Law: Preliminary draft instrument on the carriage of goods by sea - Note by the Secretariat. Ninth session, New York, 15-26 April 2002. See at <http://www.uncitral.org/english/workinggroups/wg_3/wp21e.pdf> Web page last accessed 22 March 2005.
[107] Paragraph 30, A/CN.9/WG.III/WP.21.

negotiable document even if the shipper demands it. Such behavior is justified by the fact that a negotiable document would prove to be useless (on short ferry voyages for example).[108] Requirements to contents of the document or its electronic equivalent reflect the universal practice in the industry, listing obligation to include a description of the goods. The time limitation for bringing a claim is one year and a case may be brought to carrier and the shipper alike.

What concerns **live animals** and **goods of special character**, "the carrier and any performing party" are free to "exclude or limit their liability for loss of or damage to" them. The UNCITRAL Rules are combining both the Hague and Hague-Visby way of excluding such shipments from liability, and the Hamburg Rules' approach of including such shipments with reservations.[109]

II DI revises and suplements the essential elements of carriage of goods

The UNCITRAL D.I. has approached the traditional issues concerning matters of carriage of goods by carefully pre-negotiating everything in detail. Such thorough and open discussion might in itself be considered an admirable idea. However, in order to reach an agreement, the more details there are, the more possibilities for disagreement. Rather, the value of such discussions is that it gives a comprehensive and adequate overview of the current situation (as well as possible future developments) and interests present in the industry. The following is a brief summary of currently the latest developments after 12th, 13th and 14th sessions.

Article 2[110] of version A/CN.9/WG.III/WP.32 of 12th session provides three different versions of wording for the extent of scope of the Instrument. The **scope of application**[111] would be in essence the same as in Hamburg Rules, however, in a different wording, if variant B of paragraph 1 would not suggest that the Instrument might also cover other modes of transport under certain circumstances. Thereby the Instrument becomes a 'maritime plus' Convention. Chapter 3 on

---

[108] Paragraph 126, A/CN.9/WG.III/WP.21.
Short length of the voyage also accounts for vast popularity of waybills over bills of lading in transport on the Baltic Sea. Afanasjev, Maxim.
[109] Paragraph 219, Article 17.2, A/CN.9/WG.III/WP.21.
[110] The UNCITRAL Working Group on Transport Law keeps renumbering and altering the articles.
[111] See above, pages 18 & 20 for extent of application of Hague and Hague-Visby Rules and page 23 for extent of application of Hamburg Rules.

period of responsibility obviously extends the Instrument to cover other modes of intermodal carriage. The UNCITRAL D.I. is capable of extending into a door-to-door convention.[112]

Chapter 4 of version A/CN.9/WG.III/WP.32 states the **obligations of the carrier**, which mean to essentially cover the traditional common law obligations of carrier in process of carrying goods by sea. Article 11 of the same version generally corresponds to Article III.2 of the Hague Rules and Hague-Visby Rules, setting forth the carrier's scope of duty towards the goods, which include loading, handling, stowage, carriage, keeping, caring for and discharging of goods. As a new feature, version A/CN.9/WG.III/WP.32 specifically states the opportunity to assign the aforementioned functions to be performed by or on behalf of other parties. Article 12 of version A/CN.9/WG.III/WP.32 entitles carrier to unload, destroy or render harmless dangerous goods in fear of posing actual danger to life or property. The Hague and Hague-Visby Rules' Article IV.6 and Hamburg Rules' Article 13.4 are of similar nature. Variant A of Article 12 of version A/CN.9/WG.III/WP.32 also justifies carrier's such actions if the goods are "an illegal or unacceptable danger to the environment". Article 13 of version A/CN.9/WG.III/WP.32 does not rule out the possibility of adding to the common law duty of due diligence in seaworthiness, cargoworthiness and manning, equipping and supplying the ship to "before" and "at commencement" of voyage also the duty "during" the voyage.

Chapter 5 of version A/CN.9/WG.III/WP.32 regarding **liability of the carrier** has already been modified by version A/CN.9/WG.III/WP.39 to a large extent. What concerns **basis of liability**, the Hague and Hague-Visby Rules concur that the burden of proof lies "on the person claiming the benefit of" a particular exception in the catalogue of exceptions.[113] The Draft Instrument's version A/CN.9/WG.III/WP.32 takes a similar view, whereas the Hamburg Rules have deleted the catalogue of exceptions almost entirely, leaving just the exception of fire[114]. Surprisingly, the version A/CN.9/WG.III/WP.32 lacks the exception of fire. The exception of fire was, however, put back in on the following reading. Version A/CN.9/WG.III/WP.32 confirms this on the 14th

---

[112] See above, pages 23-24 for extent of coverage of Hague, Hague-Visby and Hamburg Rules. Also see below, page 45-46 for door-to-door reference in multimodal carriage.
[113] Article IV rule 2(q) of the Hague and Hague-Visby Rules.
[114] Article 5(4)(a)(i) of the Hamburg Rules

reading.[115] The version A/CN.9/WG.III/WP.32 also reinstates the exceptions of saving life or property at sea and the exception of perils of the navigable waters. As a result of lobby of cargo interests the traditional maritime exception of negligent navigation or management of the ship has also been abolished. Quite like the Hamburg Rules, the Draft Instrument places the burden of proof on the carrier in case of a delay in delivery. The DI version A/CN.9/WG.III/WP.39 does also allow the carrier to escape liability in "reasonable attempts to avoid damage to the environment".[116]

The version A/CN.9/WG.III/WP.39 amends version A/CN.9/WG.III/WP.32 on the point of **liability of performing parties** making the carrier and the maritime performing party (not entirely unlike by Hamburg Rules) jointly and severally liable up to limits provided in the Instrument.

Whereas the Hamburg Rules state the limitation of liability of the carrier in case of a **delay**,[117] the Draft Instrument in version A/CN.9/WG.III/WP.39 goes beyond that, carefully stating what a delay is. The DI also allows for compensation of consequential loss brought on by a delay up to the "amount equivalent to one times the freight payable on the goods delayed"[118].

As of yet, the UNCITRAL Working Group on Transport Law has not settled on a specific amount for limit of liability. This makes further discussion on this subject difficult.[119] However, according to the A/CN.9/WG.III/WP.39 version the language of the Article 18 setting forth the **limits of liability** is very detailed. Article 18(2) requires highest limit of liability be applied when

---

[115] Article 22 of Draft Instrument version A/CN.9/WG.III/WP.39 – Transport Law: Preparation of a draft instrument on the carriage of goods [wholly or partly] [by sea], provisional redraft of the articles of the draft instrument considered in the report of Working Group III on the work of its thirteenth session (A/CN.9/552). Fourteenth session, Vienna, 29 November-10 December 2004. Available at: <http://daccessdds.un.org/doc/UNDOC/LTD/V04/580/33/PDF/V0458033.pdf?OpenElement> Web page last accessed 22 March 2005.
[116] Article 22 (2)(b) of Draft Instrument version A/CN.9/WG.III/WP.39.
[117] See page 13 above for what more Hamburg Rules entail on delay.
[118] Article 16(2) of Draft Instrument version A/CN.9/WG.III/WP.39.
[119] What the limit of liability is going be is likely to depend on the same factors as those that are going to be taken into consideration when amending the limit of liability in the future. In that case the Committee of representatives from each of the States Parties will look at "the experience of incidents and, in particular, the amount of damage resulting therefrom, changes in the monetary values and the effect of the proposed amendment on the cost of insurance". Article 18 bis (5). A/CN.9/WG.III/WP.39.

the place or mode of the carriage cannot be determined. Article 18(3) settles the current question[120] of whether and when a container can be considered a shipping unit stating that if goods packed in packages or shipping units are "not so enumerated, the goods in or on such container are deemed one shipping unit". The Hague-Visby Rules make generally the same statement, however, the wording gives the impression that a container is more likely to be considered a shipping unit than not.[121]

The Hague-Visby and the Hamburg Rules both state when the right to limit liability is lost (in case of a willful act or omission or recklessness with the intention or knowledge that damage would probably result).[122] So does the Draft Instrument, in its version A/CN.9/WG.III/WP.39. In the interests of greater clarity the UCNITRAL D.I. expressly places the burden of proof on the claimant.

The draft article 20 of the version A/CN.9/WG.III/WP.39, not unlike Article 19 of the Hamburg Rules, sets forth the procedure of **notifying of loss, damage or delay**. The significance of this provision is that in case the notice is not given according to provided procedure, "the carrier shall be presumed, in the absence of proof to the contrary, to have delivered the goods according to their description in the contract particulars". The notice itself may be made via electronic communication or in writing.[123] Compared to the Hamburg Rules, the time limits for various cases of inspection and notification are significantly shortened.

Version A/CN.9/WG.III/WP.39 states the requirements for a reasonable **deviation**, for which the carrier is not deemed liable. The Hague and Hague-Visby Rules concur with the Draft Instrument in their Article IV rule 4. The UNCITRAL Working Group is also seeking to include a special provision stating that a national law or a legal doctrine recognized by national law, would only have effect if the deviation is unreasonable according to the present Convention.

---

[120] David A. Glass, "The River Gurara. Containers, package limitation and the Hague Rules".
[121] Hague-Visby Rules, Article IV rule5(c).
[122] Articles IV bis (4) and 8 (1) respectively.
[123] See footnote 40 on page 9 of A/CN.9/WG.III/WP.39.

The Hague and Hague-Visby Rules have previously left the carriage of **deck cargo** unregulated. For the reason that there are special risks involved in carriage on deck, the same liability amounts should not apply. A different view was taken in the Hamburg Rules, which apply the same limitation of liability to deck cargo, if it is in accordance with the correct procedure. Version A/CN.9/WG.III/WP.39 of the Draft Instrument settle for a middle ground, setting forth the procedure to be followed for carriage of goods on deck, but imposing the same limitation of liability as for regular cargo if the goods are carried in specially fitted containers that are to be carried on deck. According to version A/CN.9/WG.III/WP.39 the carrier "shall not be liable for loss of or damage to these goods or delay in delivery caused by the special risks involved in their carriage on deck" if the goods are carried on deck according to "applicable laws or administrative rules or regulations" or in accordance with "customs, usages, and practices of the trade, or follows from other usages or practices in the trade in question".[124]

It is not stated either in Hague-Visby or Hamburg Rules what the **obligations of the shipper** in delivering the goods ready for carriage are. Article 25 of the Draft Instrument version A/CN.9/WG.III/WP.39 requires the shipper to provide goods in condition that can withstand the intended carriage and will not cause injury or damage.[125] This duty of shipper could be previously inferred from the Hague-Visby Articles IV rule 3, rule 5 (b), and Hamburg Rules Article 12. But none of the Articles clearly mention such duty, which could duly be expected of the carrier-friendlier Hague-Visby Rules. Carrier, on the other hand, has the obligation to provide information and instruction for shipper's compliance with his obligations.[126] And the shipper has the obligation to provide information, instructions and documents that are reasonably necessary for handling the goods (precautions to be taken), compliance with various rules and regulations, and for drawing up the contract particulars (ultimately for issuing the transport document). This information also includes name of the shipper and name of the consignee or order. The shipper may only refrain from such actions if he "may reasonably assume that such information is already known to the carrier".[127] The burden of proof seems to be on either of the parties to show

---

[124] Article 24 (1)(a)(c), Article 24 (2) of A/CN.9/WG.III/WP.39.
[125] The Article also requires that the shipper stow the goods in a manner that they withstand the intended journey if the goods are delivered in a container.
[126] Article 26 of A/CN.9/WG.III/WP.39.
[127] Article 27 of A/CN.9/WG.III/WP.39.

he did not give false information in case there is loss, damage, delay or injury to the goods.[128] In a case where the shipper and carrier both fail to provide the necessary information, they stand "jointly liable to the consignee or the controlling party for any such loss or damage or injury".[129]

The key factor in dealing with **dangerous goods** is shipper's duty to inform the carrier and the requirement of carrier's consent. In the case where neither of the requirements is met, the shipper is liable for "loss resulting from the shipment of such goods"[130], according to Hamburg Rules, and liability for "damages and expenses directly or indirectly arising out of such shipment"[131], according to Hague-Visby Rules. The latest version of Draft Instrument version A/CN.9/WG.III/WP.39 leans towards Hamburg Rules wording on that matter, however, adding obligations for the shipper to suitably mark the dangerous goods and inform the carrier. Similarly to Hague-Visby and Hamburg Rules, the procedure of rendering innocuous the goods in case of actual danger, is noted. The UNCITRAL D.I. also, with the help of International Convention On Liability And Compensation For Damage In Connection With The Carriage Of Hazardous And Noxious Substances By Sea, tries to define the 'dangerous goods'.[132]

The Draft Instrument also intends to define the action that states assumption of shipper's rights and obligations: at accepting or receiving the transport document or electronic record.[133] Neither has it ever been put down in an International set of Rules that the shipper is responsible for his sub-contractors, employees and agents.[134]

As I mentioned under the development process of the UNCITRAL D.I., no reference to a bill of lading is made in the Instrument for reasons explained under the same heading. However, in essence Article 33 of DI version A/CN.9/WG.III/WP.32 does provide for **issuance** of negotiable **transport documents** when goods are deemed to be "received" by the carrier. The counter arguments for this can be an express or implied agreement between the shipper and the carrier not

---

[128] Article 29 & 13 bis of A/CN.9/WG.III/WP.39.
[129] Article 29 (3) of A/CN.9/WG.III/WP.39.
[130] Article 13 (2)(a) of Hamburg Rules.
[131] Article IV rule 6 of Hague-Visby Rules.
[132] Article 30 of A/CN.9/WG.III/WP.39. footnote on page 17.
[133] Article 31 of A/CN.9/WG.III/WP.39.
[134] Article 32 of A/CN.9/WG.III/WP.39.

to use negotiable transport documents, or existence of a custom, usage or practice in trade to the contrary. Other than that there is no reason why a "received bill" cannot be issued. Issuance of electronic record goes essentially the same way.

Where the Hague, Hague-Visby and Hamburg Rules refer to contents of the bill of lading, or require a bill of lading to include, the Draft Instrument refers to **contract particulars**, which is essentially the same as those particulars need to be written on the document or electronic record.[135] The required particulars include the usual leading marks necessary for identification, number of packages or pieces, or the quantity, or weight, also the apparent order and condition of the goods.[136] The UNCITRAL D.I. also demands for information about the carrier and dates of receiving the goods, loading the goods and issuance of the transport document or electronic record. Unlike Hague-Visby and Hamburg Rules, the Draft Instrument goes on to explain what the "apparent order and condition of the goods" means. Whereas the Hamburg Rules[137] concede that there can be a situation when the carrier may not be able to inspect the goods he carries and allow for a note to be made in the bill of lading "no reasonable means of checking such particulars",[138] the Draft Instrument has adopted a more systematic approach. Article 37 of version A/CN.9/WG.III/WP.32 distinguishes between inspection of non-containerized goods and goods in closed containers. The carrier can then include in contract particulars that he had no reasonable means of checking the information provided by the shipper, and state specifically what information or characteristics he refers to.[139] Moreover, the UNCITRAL D.I. even provides a definition of reasonable means of checking, needing it to be physically practicable and commercially reasonable. In addition, it states the carrier's obligation of exercising good faith while issuing a transport document, although the burden of proof is placed "on the party claiming that the carrier did not act in good faith".[140]

---

[135] Article 34 of A/CN.9/WG.III/WP.32.
[136] The Hague-Visby Rules, Article III rule 3, the Hamburg Rules, Article 15.
[137] The Hamburg Rules contain a provision addressing this issue, the Hague and Hague-Visby Rules do not. However, it can be inferred from practice and custom that there is standard procedure for dealing with such situations. Functions as a receipt for goods shipped infers the possibility to mark down "said to contain". See page 13 above!
[138] Article 16 (1) of Hamburg Rules.
[139] Article 37 of A/CN.9/WG.III/WP.32.
[140] Article 38 of A/CN.9/WG.III/WP.32.

Just as the Hague-Visby and Hamburg Rules include an Article stating that issued bill of lading serves as **prima facie evidence of carrier's receipt** in Articles III (4) of Hague-Visby Rules and Article 16 (3)(a) of Hamburg Rules, so does the Draft Instrument in Article 39 of version A/CN.9/WG.III/WP.32, although the UNCITRAL D.I. talks of transport documents and electronic records, not of bills of lading in particular. This in essence corresponds to one of the functions of a bill of lading – **function as a receipt for goods shipped**.[141] To be precise, such function would be present if a "shipped" transport document were issued.[142] In case a "received" document is issued, it works as prima facie evidence of the goods being received.

Chapter 14 continues with **time for suit**. If it weren't for the time limit of one year like in Hague-Visby Rules[143], the provisions of the Draft Instrument[144] would be very similar to those of Hamburg Rules[145]. What also sets the UNCITRAL D.I. and Hamburg Rules apart from Hague-Visby Rules is that they talk of judicial as well as arbitral proceedings, whereas arbitral proceedings are not even mentioned in Hague-Visby Rules. However, the Draft Instrument goes further than Hamburg Rules in its detailed nature. Articles 70 and 71 set the timeframes for counterclaims and actions against bareboat charterers.

As for Chapters 15 and 16 on **jurisdiction** and **arbitration**, A/CN.9/WG.III/WP.32 provides two alternative versions, both of them based on respective provisions from Hamburg Rules. [146] Whereas the Variant A "reproduces fully the provisions of the Hamburg Rules", variant B "omits the paragraphs that the CMI International Sub-Committee on Uniformity of the Law of Carriage by Sea suggested should be deleted".[147] In Chapter 15 on jurisdiction, the CMI Sub-Committee has only omitted Article 75 (regarding new actions between the same parties on the same grounds) in Variant B, leaving Article 75 *bis*. Four places of instituting an action are given: defendant's principle place of business (or the habitual residence in the absence of the former), place of forming the contract (if the contract was made through the defendant's place of business,

---

[141] See page 13 for a more detailed discussion!
[142] Article III (7) of Hague and Hague-Visby Rules caters for this instance in particular.
[143] Article III rule 6 of Hague-Visby Rules.
[144] Article 66 Variant B, Article 67, 68 & 69 Variant B of A/CN.9/WG.III/WP.32.
[145] Article 20 of Hamburg Rules.
[146] Articles 21 & 22 of Hamburg Rules. See page 23 above for more information on jurisdiction in Hamburg rules!
[147] Footnote 222 of A/CN.9/WG.III/WP.32

branch or agency), "the place of receipt or the place of delivery"[148] or any other place noted in the transport document or electronic record for that purpose.[149]

In Chapter 16 on arbitration, the CMI Sub-Committee omitted Article 78 (on places of instituting arbitration proceedings, which correspond exactly to Article 72 stating places of instituting judicial proceedings) and Article 80 (containing a matter of reference of Articles to be included in an arbitration clause), leaving Article 80 *bis*. The Draft Instrument basically requires the agreement about arbitration to be in writing[150], the arbitration clause to be included in a negotiable transport document or a negotiable electronic record, if one has been issued[151] and the arbitrator or arbitral tribune to apply the UNCITRAL D.I.[152]. Article 80 *bis* of Variant A (same as Article 80 of Variant B) confirms that an arbitration agreement that is reached after the claim has arisen is also valid.

Since the alterations by the CMI Sub-Committee are so insignificant in Variant B, (they generally just remove repetitions) the new UNCITRAL Rules are essentially those of Hamburg Rules in either variant. The fact that the Draft Instrument relies on the Hamburg Rules in the matter of jurisdiction and arbitration is not all that surprising – neither Hague nor Hague-Visby Rules have any provisions to that effect. Moreover, the Draft Instrument is being composed by the UNCITRAL, a subdivision of United Nations, which saw to drawing up of the Hamburg Rules. In any case it is a good idea to determine a jurisdiction in the contract of carriage. Otherwise it would be left to the court seized to decide the forum and the applicable law. In deciding these matters the common law would look at terms of the contract, situation of parties and surrounding circumstances to determine the correct forum and choice of law.[153] The courts of EU Member States would be obliged to follow Council Regulation No 44/2001[154] in deciding these matters.

---

[148] Instead of this particular point, the Hamburg Rules give "the port of loading or the port of discharge". Article 21 (1) (c) of the Hamburg Rules.
[149] Article 72 of A/CN.9/WG.III/WP.32
[150] Article 76 of A/CN.9/WG.III/WP.32
[151] Article 77 of A/CN.9/WG.III/WP.32
[152] Article 79 of A/CN.9/WG.III/WP.32
[153] Wilson at p 313.
[154] Council Regulation (EC) No 44/2001 of 22 December 2000 on jurisdiction and the recognition and enforcement of judgments in civil and commercial matters. Official Journal L 012 , 16/01/2001 P. 0001 – 0023. Available at <http://europa.eu.int/eur-lex/pri/en/oj/dat/2001/l_012/l_01220010116en00010023.pdf> Website last accessed 22 March 2005.

Even knowing what the decision will be based on does not make the outcome foreseeable enough.

Chapter 17 of the UNCITRAL D.I. regulates issues of **general average**. Article V of Hague and Hague-Visby Rules are on the position that lawful provisions regarding general average are a welcome addition in a bill of lading. Article 24(1) of Hamburg Rules is of the same opinion regarding provisions to that effect in the contract of carriage or national law. Article 81 in version A/CN.9/WG.III/WP.32 reproduces this Hamburg Rules point to a tee. Article 82 (1) of the DI incorporates fully (with minor adjustments) Article 24 (2) of Hamburg Rules, which provided guidelines for a situation where consignee may refuse contribution in general average – this is subject to provisions on liability of the carrier. Article 82 (2) states for greater clarity when the time (one year)[155] for contributing to general average starts running, since the time for suit provisions do not apply to general average.[156] According to UNCITRAL D.I. version A/CN.9/WG.III/WP.32, the Working Group significantly and continuously supported the "incorporation of the York-Antwerp Rules[157] on general average into the contract of carriage".[158] This is interesting, since shipowning interests were originally against incorporating York-Antwerp Rules in shipping documents.[159]

Chapter 18 of the Draft Instrument encompasses the topic of **other conventions**. According to version A/CN.9/WG.III/WP.32 Article 83 corresponds to Article 25 (5) of Hamburg Rules and allows for other mandatorily applicable international instruments to be used in case of transport "by a mode other than carriage by sea". Articles 85 through 87 correspond to various points under Article 25 of the Hamburg Rules, concerning obligations of the carrier under "international conventions or national law governing the limitation of liability relating to the operation of ships"[160], absence of liability for luggage[161] and liability for nuclear incidents[162]. Article 84

---

[155] Time bar of one year is consistent with the amended York-Antwerp Rules of 2004. Rule XXIII. <http://www.comitemaritime.org/cmidocs/yar.html> Website last accessed 22 March 2005.
[156] Footnote 230 of A/CN.9/WG.III/WP.32.
[157] Rules by which general average losses are adjusted.
[158] Footnote 229 of A/CN.9/WG.III/WP.32.
[159] Michael Buckley, "General Average, the York-Antwerp Rules 2004." June 2004. Available at: <http://www.waltonsandmorse.com/resources/bulletins/genavg2/> Website last accessed 8 March 2005.
[160] Article 85 of version A/CN.9/WG.III/WP.32. Corresponding provision under Hamburg Rules is Article 25 (1).

stating prevalence of the instrument over earlier treaties, unless the party is not member to the instrument, was added.[163] Although the outcome remains the same, it should be noted that even though the provisions are almost identical in both Conventions, the scope of the conventions is different. The Hamburg Rules do not claim to be an intermodal Convention, whereas the UNCITRAL Instrument intends to be just that.

DI version A/CN.9/WG.III/WP.32 has two titles for Chapter 19: **limits of contractual freedom** and **contractual stipulations**. Although the footnote[164] on that particular version expresses support for the latter, it is still possible that the Working Group might decide on a third option at a later session. On some issues the Hague, Hague-Visby and Hamburg Rules concur with the Draft Instrument. Not one of them allows derogation from respective instruments and limitation or decrease of carrier's liability. Neither is insurance[165] in favor of the carrier permitted.[166] Also the increase of carrier's liability may come into question.[167] Article 89 proceeds to state that the former does not apply (the carrier and any performing party are free to exclude or limit their liability) when dealing with live animals or carriage under special agreement, subject to certain conditions.

Chapters 9 through 13 of the UNCITRAL D.I. regulate things previously unmentioned in International Rules: matters relating to general practice (the actual procedure) and known principles (such as payment of freight, delivery to consignee, right of control, transfer of rights and right of suit). Although it has been said: the more details, the more points for disagreeing, the UNCITRAL Draft seems to have recognized the need for stating the known principles and gathering them into a single document in the interest of further harmonization of carriage of goods by sea.

---

[161] Article 86 of version A/CN.9/WG.III/WP.32. Corresponding provision under Hamburg Rules is Article 25 (4).
[162] Article 87 of version A/CN.9/WG.III/WP.32. Corresponding provision under Hamburg Rules is Article 25 (3).
[163] Footnote 232 of version A/CN.9/WG.III/WP.32.
[164] Footnote 236 of version A/CN.9/WG.III/WP.32.
[165] This does not mean that carrier barred from insuring against his risks.
[166] Article III r 8 of Hague and Hague-Visby Rules, Article 23 (1) of Hamburg Rules, Article 88 of Draft Instrument. version A/CN.9/WG.III/WP.32.
[167] Article V of Hague and Hague-Visby Rules, Article 23 (2) of Hamburg Rules, Article 88 (2) of Draft Instrument. version A/CN.9/WG.III/WP.32.

Chapter 9 of the Draft Instrument lays down the rules for **freight** for the first time in an
International Convention. It merely states the general principles known for dealing with freight
stating that freight is earned "upon delivery of the goods to the consignee at the time and
location"[168] agreed for the purpose. The UNCITRAL D.I. allows for regular freight and does not
rule out advance freight. The Rules state the general principle of no set-off, "irrespective of the
cause of [...] loss, damage or failure in delivery"[169]. Article 43 (2)(b) of version
A/CN.9/WG.III/WP.39 further confirms that no contractual provision can provide the right for
the shipper to escape any monetary obligations to the carrier. The Draft also states that the carrier
is entitled to look after his interests by retaining the goods until freight and other costs[170] have
been paid for or "adequate security for such payment has provided".[171] If the carrier does not
receive his money, he is eventually entitled to sell the goods in his possession according to
procedure to cover his expenses and obtain his freight.[172]

Chapter 10 of the DI regulates **delivery to the consignee**, stating as consignee's obligation to
accept delivery of the goods and confirm the delivery of goods.[173] The delivery to the consignee
will happen upon production of proper identification if no negotiable transport document is
issued, if negotiable transport is issued, surrender of negotiable transport document is required.[174]
The UNCITRAL D.I. also provides detailed instructions in case the consignee cannot be
ascertained and the delivery cannot be made according to the original plan.[175]

Chapter 11 of the Draft Instrument's version A/CN.9/WG.III/WP.32 focuses on **right of control**.
The right of control under the Instrument means a right to give the carrier instructions in respect
of the goods, including the right to modify instructions, demand delivery of goods before their

---

[168] Article 41 of A/CN.9/WG.III/WP.32.
[169] Article 42 (2)(3) of A/CN.9/WG.III/WP.32.
[170] Those other costs can be "deadfreight, demurrage, damages for detention and all other reimbursable
costs incurred by the carrier in relation to the goods", "damages due to the carrier under the contract of
carriage", but also "any contribution in general average due to the carrier relating to the goods".
[171] Article 45 (1) of A/CN.9/WG.III/WP.32.
[172] Article 45 (2) of A/CN.9/WG.III/WP.32.
[173] Articles 46, 47 of A/CN.9/WG.III/WP.32.
[174] Articles 48, 49 of A/CN.9/WG.III/WP.32. If negotiable electronic record is issued, the holder of the
record need to verify it.
[175] Articles 49, 50 & 51 of A/CN.9/WG.III/WP.32.

arrival, replacing the consignee and agreeing to a variation of the contract of carriage with the carrier.[176] The following articles state that the shipper is the controlling party when no negotiable transport document is issued, when a negotiable transport document is issued, the controlling party is the holder. In both cases the controlling party has the right to transfer the right of control.[177]

Chapter 12 of Draft version A/CN.9/WG.III/WP.32 regulates in detail the process of **transfer of rights**. First of all, it states that in case "a negotiable transport document[178] is issued, the holder is entitled to transfer the rights in such document by passing such document to another person".[179] This, in essence, restates the transferable nature of bill of lading. On the other hand, the Chapter provides for "transfer of rights under a contract of carriage pursuant to which no negotiable transport document is issued".[180]

Chapter 13 of the UNCITRAL Draft version A/CN.9/WG.III/WP.32 sets forth who has the **rights of suit** against the carrier. The version A/CN.9/WG.III/WP.32 still has two versions of Article 63. Version A points out different parties in particular and version B gives right to take action against the carrier to "any person having a legitimate interest in the performance of any obligation arising under or in connection with such contract, where that person suffered loss or damage". However, the holder of a negotiable transport document does not need to have suffered loss or damage to assert rights under the contract of carriage.[181] But if claimant is not the holder of a negotiable transport document, he will need to "prove that the holder did not suffer the loss or damage in respect of which the claim is made" as well as "that it suffered loss or damage in consequence of a breach of the contract of carriage".[182]

---

[176] Article 53 of A/CN.9/WG.III/WP.32.
[177] Article 54 (1) (2) of A/CN.9/WG.III/WP.32. Article 54 (3) applies when a negotiable electronic record is issued.
[178] Same applies if a negotiable electronic instrument is issued. Article 59 (2) of A/CN.9/WG.III/WP.32.
[179] Article 59 (1) of A/CN.9/WG.III/WP.32.
[180] Article 61 of A/CN.9/WG.III/WP.32.
[181] Article 64 of A/CN.9/WG.III/WP.32.
[182] Article 65 of A/CN.9/WG.III/WP.32.

III Modern developments and the need to incorporate them into a single instrument

It is evident that some of the problems in carriage of goods by sea stem solely from the existence of a number of various sets of rules (creating unforeseeability as to which rules apply). The cure would be the adoption of a single set of rules, which combine the most desirable aspects of the different rules. However, there is a number of aspects which the present Rules do not regulate at all. Carriage of goods by sea has greatly benefited from technological developments in shipping that began in 1960s with the growing popularity of containerization. Although there have been attempts at regulating these advances, a uniform approach is still needed.

a) Containerization

In the second half of the twentieth century some significant changes took place that changed the way goods were transported. Container revolution[183] made shipping in containers the most efficient means of transporting goods. This meant the goods didn't have to be handled in ports and loading of containers from one mode of transport to another became rather fast and easy. Moreover, containerization facilitated multimodal transport since the containers are of a certain size, which makes handling them easy for operators of different kind of carriage and allows to set uniform standards and rates for handling them.[184]

Technological advances helped back up containers' success. Logistics systems were developed for handling containers. The ships have become faster, more precise and more reliable, which enables better planning.[185] While removing many of the problems with carriage of goods,

---

[183] Containers began to spread across the world in 1960s and 1970s. Nowadays the vast majority of liner shipping is containerized. The containers "serve as packing crate and in-transit warehouse for virtually every type of general cargo". The goods are transported in a sealed container from point of origin to the final destination. See World Shipping Council's website, "The Container Revolution". Available at <http://www.worldshipping.org/brochure/02_container_revolution.html>, and BIMCO's website, "Container shipping – logistic liners" of 5 November 2001. Available at <http://www.bimco.dk/Corporate%20Area/Seascapes/Ships%20that%20serve%20us/Container%20shippi ng%20logistic%20liners%20.aspx> Websites last accessed 1 February 2005.

[184] Jeb Anthony Clulow, "Multimodal Transport in South Africa. A Dissertation presented to the Department of Commercial Law, Faculty of Law, University of Cape Town, In partial fulfilment of the requirements for the degree of Master of Laws." Available at http://www.uctshiplaw.com/theses/clulow.htm> Website last accessed 1 February 2005.

[185] "They will typically sail on a set hour on the same day of the week, often meeting trains which will on-carry the containers, so that consignees miles inland will be able to depend upon same-day delivery in a way that has never been possible before. This reliability makes it possible for manufacturers or retailers to

containerization made it extremely difficult to determine the liability for lost or damaged cargo since it is extremely difficult to ascertain under which leg of a multimodal carriage the damage occurred.[186] As long as the Working Group has not decided on limits of liability, it is not yet entirely certain what their take on this question will be. Two possible options are the 'network' and the 'uniform' approach.[187] Article 18 (2) of the of the UNTCITRAL D.I.[188] at this point provides for a contradicting situation. The wording of the provision lets one assume that if point when damage occurred can be established, the liability limit of that mode of transport is applicable. This would be how the 'network' approach would operate. However, the Article does not expressly state so. It merely states that if the point can not be ascertained, the highest limit of liability is applied. This, on the other hand follows the principle of 'uniform' approach.

b) Electronic bills of lading

Along with the general technological advance in communication and spreading of the Internet, came the idea to administer bills of lading electronically. Electronic means is the cheapest and fastest way of communicating over distances. It would make sense to use Internet for conducting business, since so many parties (banks, insurance companies, carriers, shippers, port and customs authorities) are likely to be situated in different states.[189] Electronic bills of lading could make trade faster, administration cheaper, reduce transfer costs of paper documents and reduce fraud and security risks.[190] A major client of BOLERO system – COGSO Group – even says electronic bills of lading enables to speed up credit and can be extended to integrated logistics.[191] As one can see the advantages are persuasive. However, there are several ways of operating through electronic bills of lading.

---

greatly reduce the amount of stocks they are forced to carry, which saves substantial sums. Container shipping is a high technology, capital intensive operation, with heavy reliance on IT; computers being used to plan the stowage, to minimise handling of containers. The most modern container terminals now use a high degree of automation for movement of boxes from the shore container stack to the ship's side." See BIMCO's "Container shipping – logistic liners".

[186] Schoenbaum at p 477.

[187] The 'network' and 'uniform' approach are discussed below on page 47!

[188] See above, page 32-33 for discussion of the Article!

[189] Livermore, "Electronic Bills of Lading and Functional Equivalence", 1998 (2) The Journal of Information, Law and Technology (JILT). Available at <http://elj.warwick.ac.uk/Jilt/ecomm/98_2liv/> Website last visited 1 December 2003.

[190] "Legal Feasibility". Available at <www.bolero.net/downloads/legfeas.pdf> Website last visitied 1 December 2003.

[191] Yang Shicheng, deputy general manager of transportation division of COSCO Group. Available at <www.eyefortransport.com/archive/yahngshicheng.pdf> Website last visited 1 December 2003.

There are three main models for electronic bills of lading: CMI Rules for Electronic Bills of Lading,[192] UNCITRAL Model Law on Electronic Commerce[193] and an industry project called BOLERO[194]. Each has their advantages and disadvantages. Yet, a common characteristics that weakens them all, is their lack of legal force. The effect of the UNCITRAL Instrument incorporating provisions of electronic communication would be that they apply whenever the Instrument does. And the Instrument applies mandatorily in a number of cases (provided the State in question has adopted them). [195] If it were to become a highly popular instrument, it could harmonize yet another area of shipping law.

Drafters of the UNCITRAL Draft Instrument agreed that "the provisions covering these aspects should be technology-neutral", which means that information recorded in any medium were to be included. "Electronic record" was to refer to "contracts concluded electronically, or evidenced by messages communicated electronically".[196] The procedures with electronic transport documents[197] go essentially the same way as with paper transport documents.[198] However, at this point (and the footnote on the Draft Instrument lets one assume the position is about to change) the use of electronic communication is subject to consent of both the carrier and the shipper.[199]

c) Multimodal transport

The ship's rail no longer counts as the point where the carrier assumes liability for the goods. The liability now begins at the place the container is loaded.[200] Multimodal (or combined) transport is generally governed by door-to-door liability contracts.[201] That generally means the combined

---

[192] Comite Maritime International's Rules for Electronic Bills of Lading. Available at
<http://www.comitemaritime.org/cmidocs/rulesebla.html> Website last visited 1 February 2005.
[193] UNCITRAL Model Law on Electronic Commerce with Guide to Enactment, 1996, with additional article 5 bis as adopted in 1998. Available at <http://www.uncitral.org/english/texts/electcom/ml-ecomm.htm> Website last accessed 1 February 2005.
[194] See <http://www.bolero.net/>!
[195] See Article 2 of A/CN.9/WG.III/WP.32!
[196] See CMI's Draft Instrument on Carriage of Goods [wholly or partly][by sea].
[197] The UNCITRAL Draft Instrument does not refer to bills of lading for reasons mentioned above on pages 29-30.
[198] See Articles 33, 49, 54 of A/CN.9/WG.III/WP.32!
[199] Article 3 of A/CN.9/WG.III/WP.32!
[200] Schoenbaum at p 478.
[201] Wilson at p 241.

transport operator remains liable under a single multimodal contract for the goods during the entire transit. When successive contracts to cover each different mode are drawn, each carrier remains liable for his part of the carriage under the relevant international conventions.[202] However, whether governed by a single multimodal contract or by series of successive ones, the range of limitation of liability and of the terms between different modes of transport is very wide.

In the presence of vast variety of different Rules applicable to carriage of goods by sea in different countries, technological advances, which not have been regulated by any previous Conventions, and need for reassessing the scope of carrier liability, the idea of a new set of rules became more and more appealing. The UNCTAD International Convention on Multimodal Transport was not a success.[203] And the UNCTAD/ICC Rules did not provide efficient protection since the applicable national laws were capable of overruling contractual provisions not imposed by and international convention.

Different attempts at regulating multimodal carriage

There have been attempts to form a uniform set of rules to govern multimodal transport. UNCTAD International Convention on Multimodal Transport,[204] which was adopted in 1980, is still not in force as it hasn't received sufficient ratifications. The Convention is modelled closely on the Hamburg Rules. It would apply mandatorily to multimodal transport which either begins or ends in a Contracting State.[205] The Multimodal Convention failed to establish common monetary limits of liability.[206]

However, the International Chamber of Commerce (ICC) and UNCTAD published a set of rules[207] in 1992 that can voluntarily be applied to combined transport contracts. The ICC Rules impose the liability on combined transport operator, who is "subject to the liability regime of the

---

[202] Wilson at p 241.
[203] That could be because the Convention is based on Hamburg Rules, whereas the UNCTAD/ICC Rules are based on Hague-Visby Rules.
[204] United Nations Convention on International Multimodal Transport of Goods.
[205] Articles 2 & 3.
[206] "Bottlenecks in Door-to-Door Short Sea Shipping" at p 6. Updated 2003. Available at <http://europa.eu.int/comm/transport/maritime/sss/doc/bottlenecks-fiche-door-to-door.pdf> Website last visited 1 March 2005.
[207] UNCTAD/ICC Rules for Multimodal Transport Documents, ICC publication No. 481 (ICC, Paris, 1992).

particular mode of transport during which the loss occurred". This approach is known as the 'network' liability principle. When the point of loss can not be determined, compensation depends on the "value of the goods at the time and place they are delivered to the consignee with a limit of liability of 30 francs Poincaré[208] per kilogram of gross weight unless a different value has been declared by the shipper".[209]

There is also another approach – the 'uniform' approach, which proposes that a single regime of liability governs all modes of carriage from start of the carriage to the end.[210] When 'uniform' approach is incorporated in the contract by mutual agreement, the mandatory unimodal conventions are capable of overruling this provision in the contract.[211]

The attitude concerning the types of transport documents covering carriage in multimodal transport (in particular the voluntary UNCTAD/ICC Rules) has probably influenced the Draft Instrument's take on electronic transport documents and contributed to the deletion of bills of lading from the Instrument. Multimodal transport involving a sea leg does not necessarily need to employ a bill of lading. The parties are free to use a number of different types of documents, waybills included. Even electronic data interchange (EDI) is capable of replacing a delivery document.[212] Ocean carriers in multimodal transport may also issue an international through bill of lading, which functions like an ordinary bill of lading would. However, through a clause paramount, the carrier may subject the bill to Hague-Visby Rules, for example, which would cover the entire carriage, including parts of carriage other than by sea.[213]

According to Wilson, there is a need for highly flexible transport documents:[214]

[208] 15 francs Poincaré = 1 SDR
[209] Schoenbaum at p 488.
[210] Wilson at p 242.
[211] In practice, this has more relevance in Europe since only the sea leg may be subject to mandatory conventions outside of Europe. Wilson at p 242.
[212] Schoenbaum at p 484. Rule 2.6 of UNCTAD/ICC Rules for Multimodal Transport Documents. Reference to Incoterms 1990, ICC publication No. 460 (ICC, Paris, 1990).
[213] Schoenbaum at p 485-486.
[214] One might also think that if there is need for this kind of documents, it perhaps wouldn't be too irrational to presume there is also need for a highly extensive set of rules that can cater for all of these options, providing certain basic requirements that are consistent under different ways of transporting

"Many modern shipping documents are now drafted in a form in which they can be used interchangeably for either combined transport, through transport or on a port-to-port basis, and include terms appropriate for each contingency."[215]

The UNCITRAL Draft, at this stage, is quite liberal with its technology neutral approach, which is consistent with the current situation. It is necessary that the liberty remains.

IV Conclusion

The UNCITRAL Draft has a good chance of being the one set of Rules that ship and cargo friendly states widely adhere to. Ship friendly states might be persuaded by the fact that the CMI originally penned the draft. That the UNCITRAL Working Group took over the work and modified it to resemble the Hamburg Rules in many respects, might give confidence to states that are mainly cargo friendly. However, this might be factor that makes both sides suspicious of the Instrument. If that obstacle is overcome the UNCITRAL Working Group is capable of providing a set of Rules that is more detailed and covering widest scope of issues (including regulating the products of modern development) than any of the previous Conventions on carrier liability on carriage of goods by sea.

---

goods. This idea, however, would probably defeat the purpose of different ways of transporting goods at all, since practitioners would be robbed of choice the different options provide.
[215] Wilson at p 241.

D What would Estonia benefit from the UNCITRAL Rules?

The UNCITRAL Rules just might bring the desired certainty to benefactors of Rules governing carriage of goods by sea in Estonia. It is no longer that easy to determine whether a state is a shipowning or a cargo-owning state. The drafters in Estonia have acted with caution and let the market situation determine, which party is in a more favorable situation. In order to not create a more difficult situation for local shipowners, the carrier liability is modeled rather closely on the Scandinavian laws.

Norwegian writer Selvig recognizes that the shipping industry is undergoing significant change due to the fact that competition is much more international and a shipping country's ties to a particular country are thereby weakened. A coastal state has different roles regarding regulation on carriage of goods by sea. The liability regimes also need to take into account other factors such as country's environmental policy and export and import trade.[216]

And yet, it is general practice that States actively support transport industries by being active partners in private sector (as is the case in Finland) or by taking care of the development of the area (as is the case in Russia)[217]. In Estonia, however, the situation is different since the government of Estonia has left private enterprises to compete with developments supported by other countries' governments.[218] This, undoubtedly, can do no good to transport industry in Estonia.

These two conflicting views may perhaps be reconciled with the general notion of need for close cooperation with neighboring states. There has been talk of a possible future alliance with ports in Scandinavia and on coast of the North Sea.[219] The need for closer cooperation is equally an

---

[216] Erling Selvig, "The International Shipping Law of the Twentieth Century under Pressure" International Maritime Law, 2000, no 6, p 193.

[217] As the transit expert Raivo Vare noted in a conversation for Eesti Päevaleht's March 2004 extra 'Transiit', Russia applies a very apparent state support policy to make channels of transit more competitive.

[218] Ago Tiiman, the director of Port Operators' Association. "Eesti suurim ressurss on meie asukoht". March 2004. Transiit. Extra of Eesti Päevaleht.

[219] Meelis Atonen, Minister of Economics and Communication, "Transiit kui Eesti rahvusrikkus". March 2004. Transiit. Extra of Eesti Päevaleht.

issue within Estonia. What this dual situation means is that the competition does not go on between shipowners or freight forwarders anymore but between channels of transit, which requires a coherent internal policy as well as good relations with other parts of the channel.

Maritime law in Estonia in the Soviet Union was based on totally different principles as the maritime law in major maritime countries. Due to the hurried process, Estonian maritime law still retained similarities with the Soviet Code after regaining of independence. As a result the current Merchant Shipping Act governing carriage of goods by sea is quite recent, and takes to its Scandinavian equivalents. The recent accession to the European Union might have harmonized many other laws, yet maritime law has remained largely untouched. The accession has although contributed to stability and security in maritime law to some extent. Namely, the EU takes interest in tougher security measures and caters for recognition of judgments.

I   History and development of shipping law in Estonia

Estonia passed its Merchant Shipping Code (from now on in text also 'the Code') in 1991, December 9.[220] The Code entered into force 1 March 1992. The original Code regulated all aspects of merchant marine activities.[221] However, to this date the Code has gone through seventeen amendments, which made changes to majority of the Articles and repealed chapters VII to XXIV completely, breaking many of the topics covered under the original Code into numerous separate acts. Carriage of cargo is currently governed by Merchant Shipping Act (from now on in text also 'the Act'), which was passed 5 June of 2002 and came into force 1 October 2002.[222] As the commentary to the draft law of Merchant Shipping Act explains, the purpose of the Act is to regulate private (especially contractual) relationships that arise out of the area of merchant shipping.[223]

Erik Terk, director of Institute of Estonia's Future Studies (Eesti Tuleviku-uuringute Instituudi director). "Eesti transit 21. sajandil". March 2004. Transiit, extra to Eesti Päevaleht.
[220] State Gazette (Riigiteataja) 1991, 46/48, 577
[221] Lindpere, "Interests and Policies of Estonia in the Baltic Sea", at p 409
[222] State Gazette RT I 2002, 55, 345. Unofficial translation available at
<http://www.legaltext.ee/et/andmebaas/ava.asp?m=022>
[223] "Seletuskiri kaubandusliku meresõidu seaduse eelnõu juurde" (Commentary to the draft of Merchant Shipping Act), Section 2. Available at <http://www.just.ee/index.php3?cath=3289> Articles 1 and 2 of the Merchant Shipping Act state the purpose of the act and define merchant shipping.

48

Although it was known that the Code has several shortcomings regarding, for example, deck cargo, live animals, absence of definition of the actual carrier and lack of regulation for late delivery of goods[224], the proposed solution to these and many other problems in the shape of the Merchant Shipping Act had to wait. The work on a new act regulating merchant shipping began already in 1996. The Merchant Shipping Code of 1991 was one of the first major legislative works after regaining of independence. Because of the urgent need for it, the Code was largely based on the Soviet draft law and involved aspects solely characteristic to soviet civil law. However, the up to date Merchant Shipping Act had to wait on the completion of the Law of Obligations Act,[225] which was passed on 26 September 2001 and entered into force on 1 July 2002. Largely, the Merchant Shipping Act is *lex specialis* to the Law of Obligations Act, especially regarding contracts and carrier liability. This means the general provisions of Law of Obligations may be applicable on some occasions.[226] Yet, the carriage of goods by sea is explicitly excluded from application of Law of Obligations Act Division 1, which generally governs contracts for carriage of goods.[227]

a) Merchant Shipping Act

Commentary to the draft of Merchant Shipping Act acknowledges international nature of merchant shipping and the unification of rules through International Conventions, which leave states a relatively small area for regulation. The working group of the Merchant Shipping Act relied on the according regulations of Sweden and Finland and Hague-Visby Rules, since imposing greater liability for the carrier would render Estonian carriers less competitive in comparison to carriers of neighbouring states. Estonia decided for incorporation of the Hague-Visby Rules instead of acceding to them in case the Hamburg Rules will become popular in the Baltic Sea region.[228] Generally the Act stays true to Hague-Visby Rules, while including points

---

[224] Amos, "Vedaja vastutus rahvusvahelistel merekaubandusvedudel Haag/Visby reeglite, Hamburgi Reeglite ja Eesti kaubandusliku meresõidu koodeksi kohaselt", at p 11.
[225] State Gazette RT I 2001, 81, 487. Unofficial translation available at
<http://www.legaltext.ee/et/andmebaas/ava.asp?m=022>
[226] Commentary to the draft of Merchant Shipping Act. Section 2.
[227] According to the Commentary to the draft of Merchant Shipping Act, this is due to the tradition of marine shipping, which allows carrier to limits his liability. Article 774(3) of Law of Obligations Act provides the exception.
[228] Commentary to the draft of Merchant Shipping Act. Section 4.2.

from Hamburg Rules to govern areas previously untouched by Hague-Visby Rules such as liability of the actual carrier[229], through bill of lading.[230]

II European Union regulation of maritime law

In 2000 Erling Selvig claimed that the European Union had not entered the field of shipping law and that EU's area of regulation of shipping law was limited to protecting the four freedoms embodied in the EU Treaty.[231] That, to a very large extent, is still the case. A definite priority seems to be putting maritime transport into accordance with the basic principles of Community law (freedom to provide services, competition, unfair pricing practices and free access to ocean trade).[232] A number of Regulations[233] and court cases[234] speak to that effect.

In addition to that, the EU is concerned about maritime safety, which became an issue after the Erika and the Prestige oil spills. Therefore, the European Commission is interested in "tougher ship inspections, sanctions for pollution caused through gross negligence, and the accelerated phasing out of single-hulled tankers".[235] Among other things[236] White Paper 2001 further

---

[229] Article 34 of Merchant Shipping Act.
[230] Article 44 of Merchant Shipping Act.
[231] Erling Selvig, "The International Shipping Law of the Twentieth Century under Pressure", International Maritime Law, 2000, no 6, p 191.
[232] "Freedom to supply services, competition, unfair pricing practices and free access to ocean trade." Last updated: 07.02.2003.Available at <http://europa.eu.int/scadplus/leg/en/lvb/l24064.htm> Web page last visited 1 February 2005.
[233] Regulations 4055/86 applying the principle of freedom to provide services to maritime transport (Official Journal L 378, 31/12/1986 P. 0001 – 0003), 4056/86 laying down detailed rules for the application of Article 85 and 86 of the Treaty to maritime transport (Official Journal L 378, 31/12/1986 P. 0004 – 0013), 4057/86 on unfair pricing practices in maritime transport (Official Journal L 378, 31/12/1986 P. 0014 – 0020), 4058/86 concerning coordinated action to safeguard free access to cargoes in ocean trades (Official Journal L 378, 31/12/1986 P. 0021 - 0023 Finnish special edition: Chapter 7 Volume 3 P. 0148 Swedish special edition: Chapter 7 Volume 3 P. 0148) and 3577/92 applying the principle of freedom to provide services to maritime transport within Member States (Official Journal L 364, 12/12/1992 P. 0007 - 0010 Finnish special edition: Chapter 6 Volume 3 P. 0203 Swedish special edition: Chapter 6 Volume 3 P. 0203).
[234] Cases C-288/02: Commission of the European communities v Hellenic Republic 1, European court reports 2004; C-435/00: Geha Naftiliaki EPE and Others v NPDD Limeniko Tameio DOD/SOU and Elliniko Dimosio, European Court reports 2002, page I-10615; Joined Cases C-430/99 and C-431/99: Inspecteur van de Belastingdienst Douane, district Rotterdam v Sea-Land Service Inc. and Nedlloyd Lijnen BV, European Court reports 2002, page I-05235, deal with freedom to provide services.
[235] Overview of the European Union Activities, Transport. Last updated: June 2004. Available at <http://europa.eu.int/pol/trans/overview_en.htm> Web page last visited 1 February 2005.
[236] However, the White paper also provided for more investments in maritime and inland waterways and port services.

provided for higher maritime safety standards.[237] Regulation 1406/2002 established the European Maritime Safety Agency, which has "legal competence and the necessary means to combat pollution by ships".[238]

Those steps can also be seen as a measure for fighting the phenomenon of flagging out, which is a "drift of the EU fleet towards "flags of convenience"[...] countries which are far more attractive to shipowners than Europe in terms of taxation, social legislation and safety or environment standards."[239] The problem with flagging out is that it causes nearly half of the jobs to be lost.[240]

Other than maritime law concerning basic principles of Community law and higher standards for maritime safety, the EU does essentially keep itself out of other issues of maritime law, including the regulation of carriage of goods by sea. Such approach by the EU is frankly surprising since maritime transport in the Union is no insignificant matter. The sheer volume of goods – "more than 1 billion tones of freight a year" are handled in EU ports, and the percentage – "over 90% of its external trade and some 43% of its internal trade goes by sea" – are impressive figures even by the most modest standards. In addition to that, "Maritime companies belong[ing] to European Union nationals control one third of the world fleet, and some 40% of EU trade is carried on vessels controlled by EU interests."[241]

Moreover, the EU combines a number of different legal systems, and it would be logical to infer that this alone can cause additional costs and confusion in carriage of goods by sea. This issue seems to be both acknowledged and ignored.[242]

---

[237] "Overview of the European Union Activities, Transport."
[238] "General Report 2003 - Chapter V: Citizenship and quality of life. Section 6: Transport (21/47)." Last update: 07-02-2004. Available at <http://europa.eu.int/abc/doc/off/rg/en/2003/pt0683.htm#anch0350> Website last visited 1 February 2005.
[239] "Overview of maritime transport policy." Last update: 26-10-2004. Available at <http://europa.eu.int/comm/transport/maritime/index_en.htm> Website last visited 1 February 2005.
[240] "Overview of maritime transport policy."
[241] "Overview of maritime transport policy."
[242] "The free movement of vessels is also hampered by the diversity of legal systems with different rules, particularly on technical specifications for vessels and pilots' certificates." White Paper – European transport policy for 2010: time to decide. Available at

However, multimodal or combined transport (also known as 'intermodality), has been in Community's attention for a while already[243] (1997: PACT [Pilot Action for Combined Transport] programme was to promote the use of combined transport)[244] as the EU hoped it to solve its problem with overexploitation of road carriage and congestion.[245] The PACT programme was then replaced by the Marco Polo Programme, which similarly states its aim to be "shift[ing] freight from the roads to more environmentally friendly modes".[246]

It was soon noticed that in order for the intermodality to function, technical measures on containers and loading units would have to be unified.[247] Conventional shipping containers were "too narrow to accommodate two standard pallets side by side". In addition to that, the "containers used by US or Asian companies exporting all over the world would pose safety problems on European roads".[248] The work on harmonization of Intermodal Loading Units is currently underway. The amended proposal of Directive 96/53 was presented on 30 April 2004.[249]

<http://europa.eu.int/comm/energy_transport/library/lb_texte_complet_en.pdf> Web page last visited 1 February 2005.
[243] Council Directive 92/106/EEC, Article 1 gave the definition of "combined transport" as early as 7 December 1992.
Council Directive 92/106/EEC of 7 December 1992 on the establishment of common rules for certain types of combined transport of goods between Member States. Official Journal L 368, 17/12/1992 P. 0038 – 0042. Available at
<http://europa.eu.int/smartapi/cgi/sga_doc?smartapi!celexplus!prod!CELEXnumdoc&lg=en&numdoc=31 992L0106> Website last visited 1 February 2005.
[244] "Combined transport: PACT programme (1997-2001)". Last updated: 12.08.2002. Available at <http://europa.eu.int/scadplus/leg/en/lvb/l24172.htm> Website last visited 1 February 2005.
[245] "Europe at a crossroads. The need for sustainable transport." Available at
<http://europa.eu.int/comm/publications/booklets/move/39/en.pdf> Website last visited 1 February 2005.
Later, in the Commissions White Paper: European Transport Policy for 2010, the aim of building transport chains that are more efficient, cost effective and sustainable, was also added.
[246] "Combined transport: The Marco Polo Programme." Last updated: 06.09.2004. Available at <http://europa.eu.int/scadplus/leg/en/lvb/l24159.htm> Web page last visited 1 February 2005.
[247] "White Paper – European transport policy for 2010: time to decide."
[248] "White Paper – European transport policy for 2010: time to decide."
[249] "Proposal for a Directive of the European Parliament and of the Council on Intermodal Loading Units", 07/04/2003. See at
<http://europa.eu.int/comm/transport/intermodality/legislation/doc/acte_com_2003_155_en.pdf> Website last visited 1 February 2005.

III Recognition of judgments

Luckily, the European Union does provide for easier recognition and enforcement of judgments through the Council Regulation No 44/2001.[250] The Regulation revises the Brussels and Lugano Conventions on Jurisdiction and Enforcement of Judgments in Civil and Commercial Matters.[251] As Estonia is a Member State, the Regulation is directly and entirely applicable.[252] Since Estonia became a Member State of the European Union less than a year ago – on 1 May 2004, the effectiveness of the Council Regulation in Estonia is yet to be put to the test.

IV General average and insurance

General average and insurance are two different ways of recovering compensation for lost or damaged goods. Whereas general average applies automatically, insurance contracts have to be concluded. Since general average is part of maritime custom and law, it is subject to carrier's right to limit his responsibility. Therefore, sum recovered is usually lower than the value of goods. Additionally, general average is meant to cover not only damage or loss of goods but also damage suffered by the ship (ship repairs, toeing). This is why it is a good idea to insure the goods.[253] Moreover, some insurance policies allow recovery for economic loss (the value of the goods may be higher in the point of destination).[254]

According to the director of Maritime Cargo Estonia OÜ Aare Kaarma, the shippers in Estonia generally do not insure their goods since general average only comes "across in practice about once in five years" and insurance is considered "expensive when it is 0,5% of the value of goods".[255] According to the director of GC Cargomasters Raido Rebane, the "clients are not acquainted with the first part of the Bill of Lading".[256] Thereby, they are uninformed as to which

---

[250] Council Regulation (EC) No 44/2001 of 22 December 2000 on jurisdiction and the recognition and enforcement of judgments in civil and commercial matters. Official Journal L 012 , 16/01/2001 P. 0001 – 0023. Available at <http://europa.eu.int/eur-lex/pri/en/oj/dat/2001/l_012/l_01220010116en00010023.pdf> Website last accessed 22 March 2005.
[251] The Brussels Convention concluded between the Member States on 27 September 1968 and the Lugano Convention concluded between the Member States and EFTA States on 16 September 1988.
[252] Article 249 of European Community Treaty.
[253] Rivo Sarapik, "Kaubakindlustus annab mereveol raha tagasi", Äripäev, 27 January 2003. Available at <http://www.ergofondid.ee/txt/pages/ERGOpe000846> Website last accessed 21 July 2004.
[254] "Kindlustus." IK Speditor Group Website. Available at
<http://www.ik.ee/index.php?lang=est&main_id=1,20> Website last accessed 1 February 2005.
[255] Sarapik
[256] Sarapik

Rules govern the carriage. For example, the TECO Lines' liner bill of lading incorporates CONLINEBILL[257] terms of 1950, which have been amended several times, though last time in 1978. The CONLINEBILL as stated on the back of TECO Lines' liner bill of lading applies the Hague or Hague-Visby Rules and declares the jurisdiction to be the country of the carrier's principle place of business, and the law applicable in that state. Since TECO is the carrier and its principle place of business is in Estonia, the forum is in Estonia and the applicable law Estonian legislation along with the Merchant Shipping Act, which may at times slightly depart from the CONLINEBILL. Though, like CONLINEBILL, the Merchant Shipping Act of Estonia refers to York-Antwerp Rules in division of expenditure and on determination of the size of it.[258] The International Conventions delegate the right to refer to Rules or Conventions regulating general average to national laws[259]

V Conclusion

The actual benefit of the UNCITRAL Instrument for Estonia may remain hidden since incidents that require legal interference are quite rare. Most of the time the business goes on without any sign of the actual legislation behind it. Clients are often uninformed as to which Rules govern the carriage. To this day, there is no case history in Estonia to try out the Estonian Merchant Act in practice. However, being a part of universally successful set of Rules governing carrier liability, would also attribute trust and reliability to Estonia in the eyes of foreign parties involved in business undertakings in Estonia. And besides the desired uniformity, the UNCITRAL Instrument responds to the trends in the industry. It caters for electronic documents, containers and multimodal carriage. Although the Estonian Act is quite recent, the UNCITRAL Rules is even younger. Even a few years are capable of making a remarkable difference.

---

[257] Liner terms approved by the Baltic and International Maritime Conference. See Appendix for the TECO Line's liner bill of lading!
[258] §122 (Definiton of general average). Estonian Merchant Shipping Act.
[259] The UNCITRAL Draft Instrument, Article 81. The Hamburg Rules, Article 24(1). The Hague and Hague-Visby Rules, Article V phrases it 'lawful provisions'. See also above, page 39!

E Some new ideas

When the objective is harmonization of Rules that apply with a legal force, there is not a wide selection of solutions available. An International Convention is best placed to achieve this aim. However, the way this Convention is drafted, what it contains and how it is implemented, can change the outcome and the success of it.

Although the UCNITRAL Working Group on Transport Law includes people that are maritime experts, International Associations still remain removed from the industry. And this is the project that needs involvement and interest of the industry, if it is to be successful. If the industry really needs a single set of Rules to unite under, it should start working from what works in practice towards eliminating the hindrances caused by discrepancies of law. An industry project with a fresh approach that justifies itself by gathering increasing popularity (like the Bolero project) would be one option. The working formula could then be formed into an International Convention or given the force of law in some other way. However, it is not likely that any project will become overwhelmingly popular. Even if it did, this solution would take a lot of time.

The UNCITRAL Draft Instrument aims to be an intermodal Convention. Inevitably, other modes of carriage are affected. The present Draft attempts to regulate matters by providing its own provisions. It could also delegate some of its responsibility to other Conventions. There are some severe risks to that approach – great reliance on other Conventions and possible conflicts.

However, sorting out the maritime law problems is only the first step in working out an intermodal Convention. Even though, the focus is on producing a 'maritime plus' convention that would only apply to other modes of carriage if a sea leg is involved, it shouldn't be expected that parties involved in other modes of carriage should agree with such arrangements. Perhaps unfairly, significantly lower liability limits would then apply to carriers of other modes.

The drafters of the New Rules have overlooked (or perhaps not yet decided on) the implementation of the Rules. The attempt to unify outcome of litigation in contracting states of the Hague Rules failed because of the different ways Rules were brought into force.[260] The UNCITRAL Rules should be made to apply in the same way in all of Contracting States.

F Conclusion

The importance of trade is difficult to underestimate. There are no signs of decrease in the carriage of goods globally. One of the most cost-effective ways of transporting goods across long distances is carriage by sea. Although the likelihood of accidents that result in damage or loss of cargo is small, a small percentage of a vast overall sum, however, results in a noticeable quantity. And when it does happen, noticeable amount of money is at stake.

In certain circumstances (when the port of departure is in a state where Hague or Hague-Visby Rules apply, and the port of destination is in a state where Hamburg Rules apply) the confusion is inevitable if the goods suffer damage or are lost, since the contract of carriage is automatically covered by Rules the parties never intended to apply. The ever unpredictable law of forum selection process is then begun. Depending on the forum caught, the applicable law is decided on. And depending on Rules applicable under the law, and also the way the Rules are incorporated, the final applicable law is found. This "equation with several 'unknowns'" is both costly and time consuming. The parallel existence of the Hague, Hague-Visby and Hamburg Rules, all of which apply different limits of liability for the carrier is becoming more and more of a problem.

A number of parallel Rules on carrier liability is not the only problem. Another problem is the datedness of the Rules. There are no amendments made to any of the existing International Conventions on carrier liability since 1978, when the Hamburg Rules were adopted. The UNCITRAL Draft Instrument revises and completes the already existing International Conventions on carrier liability. The Instrument provides provisions on carriage under electronic documents and gives the updated approach on containerisation. Also, the instrument intends to cover other modes of carriage besides the sea leg, stretching itself into a multimodal Convention.

---

[260] See above, pages 17-18!

The problems present in the industry can mainly be solved through an International Convention, or alternatively through an industry project. What make agreements so problematic are the opposing interests of shippers and carriers. Therefore, the solution could either be a complete and universal agreement or a somewhat painful compromise. A complete and universal agreement is perhaps possible as a result of longstanding practice and cooperation. However, as a likely solution, capable to come into effect in a couple of years, the UNCITRAL Draft Instrument is a realistic chance for the desired goal. The UNCITRAL Instrument originating from the CMI might persuade both ship and cargo friendly states that their interests are adequately represented. It might also make both the sides suspicious of the new Rules. Whichever way it goes, it is then the measure of urgency and actual need for a solution.

Although relevant to me, because I am an Estonian citizen, the example of maritime law and practice in Estonia, is not very relevant to the discussion of the UNCITRAL Draft. Due to political and legislative circumstances, it is not possible to give an overview of merits and shortcomings of maritime law in Estonia. Neither is it possible to draw any adequate conclusions what Estonia could benefit from the new UNCITRAL Rules. However, likely advantages can be gathered: such as contributions to commercial stability and increased interest from foreign traders. Even on the Baltic Sea, the trade does not only take place between European Union Member States.

The UNCITRAL Instrument is still in the process of being drafted. The actual discussion on a liability limit has not even officially begun. And my thesis has been a hypothetical discussion addressing the points where existing Rules and the UNCITRAL Draft Instrument depart, and pointing to provisions they share. Not one version of the Draft consistently refers to the specific differences and similarities. My thesis barely scratches the surface. However, I would recommend the Working Group a similar method of systematically going through all the information regarding all of the liability Rules to ascertain which side favours which approach and more importantly why. That way the UNCITRAL Rules on carriage of goods by sea wouldn't necessarily have to be a somewhat painful compromise.

Summary

In this Thesis I set out to prove that the shipping industry is in need of a single set of rules governing carrier liability due to unforeseeability created by presence of multiple liability regimes. The UNCITRAL Draft Instrument is currently the best solution for the problem. The UNCITRAL D.I. balances the interests of shippers and carriers, revises and perfects the existing International Rules governing carriage of goods by sea. It also incorporates previously unregulated modern developments into a single Instrument.

Bibliography

Books and Independent Publications

- August, Ray. "International Business Law. Text, cases, and readings". 2000, 3rd ed, Prentice Hall
- Falkanger, Thor, Bull & Brautaset. "Scandinavian maritime law. The Norwegian perspective". 2004, 2nd ed, Universitetsforlaget
- Grime, Robert. "Shipping Law". 1991, second edition, London, Sweet & Maxwell
- Schoenbaum, Thomas J. "Admiralty and Maritime Law". 1994, 2nd edition, West Publishing Co.
- Wilson, John F. "Carriage of Goods by sea". 2001, 4th edition, Pearson Education Limited

Articles and Contributions to Edited Works

- Amos, Mari, "Vedaja vastututs rahvusvahelistel merekaubandusvedudel Haag-Visby reeglite, Hamburgi reeglite ja Eesti kaubandusliku meresõidu koodeksi kohaselt" *Õigusinstituudi Toimetised*, 1999 sügis, p 9-11
- Baughen, Simon, "Defining the Ambit of Article III r.8 of the Hague Rules; Obligations and Exceptions Clauses" *Journal of International Maritime Law*, 9, 2003, 2, p 115-122
- Clarke, Malcolm, "A conflict of conventions: The UNCITRAL/CMI draft transport instrument on your doorstep" *Journal of International Maritime Law*, 2003, no 1, p 28-39
- Davis, Ian, "COGSA 98: The Australian Carriage of Goods by Sea Act" *International Maritime Law*, 1998, 7, p 223-227
- Force, Robert, "Under the US Carriage of Goods by Sea Act, a container may not be a package even where the bill of lading says that it is" *International Maritime Law*, 1995, 2, p 13-15
- Glass, David A, "The River Gurara. Containers, package limitation and the Hague Rules" *Shipping and Transport Lawyer*, Volume 1 Number 1, p 10-12.
- Lindpere, Heiki, "Aktuaalseid probleeme Eesti Vabariigi kaasaegses mereõiguses" *Juridica*, III/2000, p 178-181

- Lindpere, Heiki, "Interests and Policies of Estonia in the Baltic Sea"
  The Baltic Sea: New Developments in National Policies and International Cooperation,
  edited by Platzöder & Verlaan,1996, p 407-410
- Mildon, David, "Carriage of Goods by Sea: Statutory Reforms which Meet in Unexpected Places"
  International Maritime Law, 1995, 5, p 139-145
- Pejovic, Caslav, "Delivery of goods without a bill of lading: revival of an old problem in the Far East"
  Journal of International Maritime Law, 9, 2003, 5, p 448-460
- Pejociv, Caslav, "Documents of Title in Carriage of Goods by Sea: Present Status and Possible Future Directions"
  The Journal of Business Law, 2001, September issue, p 461-488
- Selvig, Erling, "The International Shipping Law of the Twentieth Century under Pressure"
  International Maritime Law, 2000, no 6, p 190-195
- Sturley, Michael F., "Scope of coverage under the UNCITRAL Draft Instrument"
  Journal of International Maritime Law, 2004, no 2, p 138-154
- Tetley, William, Q.C., "Interpretation and Construction of the Hague, Hague/Visby and Hamburg Rules"
  Journal of International Maritime Law, 10, 2004, 1, p 30-70

Internet sources

Comite Maritime International's website
- Comite Maritime International "A Brief Structural History of the First Century"
  Available at <http://www.comitemaritime.org/histo/his.html> Website last visited 1 February 2005.
- Comite Maritime International "Draft Instrument on Carriage of Goods [wholly or partly] [by sea]"
  Available at <http://www.comitemaritime.org/draft/draft.html> Website last accessed 1 February 2005.
- Comite Maritime International "Rules for Electronic Bills of Lading"

Available at <http://www.comitemaritime.org/cmidocs/rulesebla.html> Website last visited 1 February 2005.

- "Status of ratifications of Maritime Conventions. United Nations Convention on the Carriage of Goods by sea. Hamburg, 31 March 1978"
Available at <http://www.comitemaritime.org/ratific/uninat/uni02.html> Website last accessed 1 February 2005.

European Union's website

- "Bottlenecks in Door-to-Door Short Sea Shipping" Updated 2003.
Available at <http://europa.eu.int/comm/transport/maritime/sss/doc/bottlenecks-fiche-door-to-door.pdf> Website last visited 1 March 2005.

- "Combined transport: PACT programme (1997-2001)" Last updated: 12.08.2002.
Available at <http://europa.eu.int/scadplus/leg/en/lvb/l24172.htm> Website last visited 1 February 2005.

- "Combined transport: The Marco Polo Programme" Last updated: 06.09.2004.
Available at <http://europa.eu.int/scadplus/leg/en/lvb/l24159.htm> Web page last visited 1 February 2005.

- "Europe at a crossroads. The need for sustainable transport"
Available at <http://europa.eu.int/comm/publications/booklets/move/39/en.pdf> Website last visited 1 February 2005.

- "Freedom to supply services, competition, unfair pricing practices and free access to ocean trade" Last updated: 07.02.2003.
Available at <http://europa.eu.int/scadplus/leg/en/lvb/l24064.htm> Web page last visited 1 February 2005.

- "General Report 2003 - Chapter V: Citizenship and quality of life. Section 6: Transport" (21/47). Last update: 07-02-2004.
Available at <http://europa.eu.int/abc/doc/off/rg/en/2003/pt0683.htm#anch0350> Website last visited 1 February 2005.

- "Overview of maritime transport policy" Last update: 26-10-2004.
Available at <http://europa.eu.int/comm/transport/maritime/index_en.htm> Website last visited 1 February 2005

- "Overview of the European Union Activities, Transport" Last updated: June 2004. Available at <http://europa.eu.int/pol/trans/overview_en.htm> Web page last visited 1 February 2005.
- "Proposal for a Directive of the European Parliament and of the Council on Intermodal Loading Units" 07/04/2003.
  Available at
  <http://europa.eu.int/comm/transport/intermodality/legislation/doc/acte_com_2003_155_e n.pdf> Website last visited 1 February 2005.
- "White Paper – European transport policy for 2010: time to decide"
  Available at
  <http://europa.eu.int/comm/energy_transport/library/lb_texte_complet_en.pdf> Web page last visited 1 February 2005.

Tetley's maritime and admiralty law website

- Tetley, William, Q.C., "Chapter 1, Application of the Rules generally" Available at <http://upload.mcgill.ca/maritimelaw/ch1marine.pdf> Website last accessed 13 March 2005.
- Tetley, William, Q.C., "Interpretation and Construction of the Hague, Hague/Visby and Hamburg Rules" (published in 2004) 10 JIML 30-70.
  Available at <http://upload.mcgill.ca/maritimelaw/rulesinterpretation.pdf> Website last accessed 13 March 2005.
- Tetley, William, Q.C., "Reform of Carriage of Goods – the UNCITRAL Draft and Senate COGSA'99"
  Tulane Maritime Law Journal, Winter 2003.
  Available at <http://upload.mcgill.ca/maritimelaw/uncitralcogsareform.pdf> Web page last accessed 13 March 2005.

The UCITRAL Working Group on Transport Law Drafts

- A/CN.9/WG.III/WP.39 – Transport Law: Preparation of a draft instrument on the carriage of goods [wholly or partly] [by sea], provisional redraft of the articles of the draft instrument considered in the report of Working Group III on the work of its thirteenth session (A/CN.9/552). Fourteenth session, Vienna, 29 November-10 December 2004. Available at:

<http://daccessdds.un.org/doc/UNDOC/LTD/V04/580/33/PDF/V0458033.pdf?OpenElem ent> Web page last accessed 22 March 2005.

- A/CN.9/WG.III/WP.32 – Transport Law: Draft instrument on the carriage of goods [wholly or partly] [by sea] - Note by the Secretariat. Twelfth session, Vienna, 6-17 October 2003. Available at: <http://www.uncitral.org/english/workinggroups/wg_3/WP32-FINAL%20REVISION%203%20Sept.pdf> Web page last accessed 22 March 2005.
- A/CN.9/WG.III/WP.21 – Transport Law: Preliminary draft instrument on the carriage of goods by sea - Note by the Secretariat. Ninth session, New York, 15-26 April 2002. Available at: <http://www.uncitral.org/english/workinggroups/wg_3/wp21e.pdf> Web page last accessed 22 March 2005.

Other

- BIMCO. "Container shipping – logistic liners" 05 November 2001. Available at <http://www.bimco.dk/Corporate%20Area/Seascapes/Ships%20that%20serve%20us/Con tainer%20shipping%20logistic%20liners%20.aspx> Website last accessed 1 February 2005.
- Buckley, Michael. "General Average, the York-Antwerp Rules 2004" June 2004. Available at: <http://www.waltonsandmorse.com/resources/bulletins/genavg2/> Website last accessed 8 March 2005.
- Clulow, Jeb Anthony. "Multimodal Transport in South Africa. A Dissertation presented to the Department of Commercial Law, Faculty of Law, University of Cape Town, In partial fulfilment of the requirements for the degree of Master of Laws" Available at http://www.uctshiplaw.com/theses/clulow.htm> Website last accessed 1 February 2005.
- "Kindlustus" IK Speditor Group Website. Available at <http://www.ik.ee/index.php?lang=est&main_id=1,20> Website last accessed 1 February 2005.
- "Legal Feasibility" Available at <www.bolero.net/downloads/legfeas.pdf> Website last visitied 1 December 2003.

- Livermore J et al, 'Electronic Bills of Lading and Functional Equivalence', 1998 (2) The Journal of Information, Law and Technology (JILT).
  Available at <http://elj.warwick.ac.uk/Jilt/ecomm/98_2liv/> Website last visited 1 December 2003.
- "Medieval Sourcebook: Bill of Lading, 1248"
  Available at <http://www.fordham.edu/halsall/source/1248billoflading.html> Website last accessed 22 October 2004.
- Sarapik, Rivo. "Kaubakindlustus annab mereveol raha tagasi" Äripäev, 27 January 2003.
  Available at <http://www.ergofondid.ee/txt/pages/ERGOpe000846> Website last accessed 21 July 2004.
- "Seletuskiri kaubandusliku meresõidu seaduse eelnõu juurde" (Commentary to the draft of Merchant Shipping Act)
  Available at <http://www.just.ee/index.php3?cath=3289> Website last accessed 1 February 2005.
- Shicheng, Yang, deputy general manager of transportation division of COSCO Group.
  Available at <www.eyefortransport.com/archive/yahngshicheng.pdf> Website last visited 1 December 2003.
- "UNCITRAL Model Law on Electronic Commerce with Guide to Enactment, 1996, with additional article 5 bis as adopted in 1998"
  Available at <http://www.uncitral.org/english/texts/electcom/ml-ecomm.htm> Website last accessed 1 February 2005.
- "UN Hamburg Rules of 1978" Website of Organisation for Economic Co-operation and Development.
  Available at
  <http://www.oecd.org/document/13/0,2340,en_2649_34337_1866253_119666_1_1_1,00.html> Website last accessed 1 February 2005.
- World Shipping Council. "The Container Revolution"
  Available at <http://www.worldshipping.org/brochure/02_container_revolution.html> Website last accessed 1 February 2005.

Cases

European Court of Justice

- Case C-288/02: Commission of the European Communities v Hellenic Republic 1 European Court reports 2004, Page 00000.
- C-435/00: Geha Naftiliaki EPE and Others v NPDD Limeniko Tameio DOD/SOU and Elliniko Dimosio
  European Court reports 2002, Page I-10615
- Joined Cases C-430/99 and C-431/99: Inspecteur van de Belastingdienst Douane, district Rotterdam v Sea-Land Service Inc. and Nedlloyd Lijnen BV.
  European Court reports 2002, Page I-05235

National courts – Great Britain

- Pyrene Co. V. Scindia Navigaton Co., Ltd [1954] 2 QB 402 at pp 419-420, [1954] 1 Lloyd's Rep. 321 at p 329.
- Effort shipping Co. Ltd. V Linden Management S.A. [1998] 1 Lloyd's Rep. 337 at p. 346, 1998 AMC 1050 at p. 1065 (H.L.)

Table of Legislative acts

European Union

- Treaty Establishing the European Community, signed 25 March 1957, came into force 1 January 1958. The consolidated version, Official Journal C 325 , 24 December 2002
- Council Regulation (EC) No 44/2001 of 22 December 2000 on jurisdiction and the recognition and enforcement of judgments in civil and commercial matters. Official Journal L 012 , 16/01/2001 P. 0001 – 0023. Available at <http://europa.eu.int/eur-lex/pri/en/oj/dat/2001/l_012/l_01220010116en00010023.pdf> Website last accessed 22 March 2005.
- Council Regulation (EEC) No 4055/86 of 22 December 1986 applying the principle of freedom to provide services to maritime transport between Member States and between Member States and third. Official Journal L 378, 31/12/1986 P. 0001 – 0003.
- Council Regulation (EEC) No 4056/86 of 22 December 1986 laying down detailed rules for the application of Articles 85 and 86 of the Treaty to maritime transport. Official Journal L 378, 31/12/1986 P. 0004 – 0013.

- Council Regulation (EEC) No 4057/86 of 22 December 1986 on unfair pricing practices in maritime transport. Official Journal L 378 , 31/12/1986 P. 0014 – 0020.
- Council Regulation (EEC) No 4058/86 of 22 December 1986 concerning coordinated action to safeguard free access to cargoes in ocean trades. Official Journal L 378 , 31/12/1986 P. 0021 - 0023 Finnish special edition: Chapter 7 Volume 3 P. 0148 Swedish special edition: Chapter 7 Volume 3 P. 0148.
- Council Regulation (EEC) No 3577/92 of 7 December 1992 applying the principle of freedom to provide sevices to maritime transport within Member States (maritime cabotage). Official Journal L 364 , 12/12/1992 P. 0007 - 0010 Finnish special edition: Chapter 6 Volume 3 P. 0203 Swedish special edition: Chapter 6 Volume 3 P. 0203.
- Council Directive 92/106/EEC of 7 December 1992 on the establishment of common rules for certain types of combined transport of goods between Member States. Official Journal L 368, 17/12/1992 P. 0038 – 0042. Available at <http://europa.eu.int/smartapi/cgi/sga_doc?smartapi!celexplus!prod!CELEXnumdoc&lg=en&numdoc=31992L0106> Website last visited 1 February 2005.

International Agreements and Conventions

- International Convention for the Unification of Certain Rules of Law relating to Bills of Lading ("Hague Rules"), and Protocol of Signature. Signed in Brussels, 25 August 1924. Available at <www.admiraltylawguide.com/conven/haguerules1924.html>
- Protocol to Amend the International Convention for the Unification of Certain Rules of Law Relating to Bills of Lading ("Visby Rules"). Signed in Brussels, 23 February 1968. Available at <www.admiraltylawguide.com/conven/visbyrules1968.html>
- The Hague-Visby Rules. The Hague Rules as Amended by the Brussels Protocol 1968 Available at <www.forwarderlaw.com/archive/visby.htm>
- Protocol (SDR Protocol) amending the International Convention for the Unification of Certain Rules of Law relating to Bills of Lading of 25 August 1924 (The Hague Rules), as amended by the Protocol of 23 February 1968 (Visby Rules). Signed in Brussels, 21 December 1979)
  Available at <http://www.admiraltylawguide.com/conven/sdrprotocol1979.html>

- United Nations Convention on the Carriage of Goods by Sea ("Hamburg Rules"). Signed in Hamburg, 31 March 1978.
  Available at <www.admiraltylawguide.com/conven/hamburgrules1978.html>
- The York-Antwerp Rules of 2004. Available at <http://www.comitemaritime.org/cmidocs/yar.html> Website last accessed 22 March 2005.

National laws

- Kaubandusliku meresõidu koodeks (Merchant Shipping Code). Passed on 9 December 1991 (RT I 1991, 46/48, 577), amended by (RT I 2004, 46, 329; RT I 2004, 30, 208; RT I 2004, 24, 164; RT I 2003, 88, 594; RT I 2002,1,1; RT I 2002, 55, 345; RT I 2001, 93, 565; RT I 2001, 21, 114; RT I 2000, 35, 221; RT I 1998, 30, 409; RT I 1998, 23, 321; RT I 1998, 2, 47; RT I 1997, 77, 1315; RT I 1996, 78, 1380; RT I 1995, 54, 882). The current version of the code. Available along with the unofficial translation at <www.legaltext.ee/et/andmebaas/ava.asp?m=022>
  Available at <http://www.riigiteataja.ee/ert/act.jsp?id=769218> Web page last accessed 13 March 2005.
- Kaubandusliku meresõidu seadus (Merchant Shipping Act) Passed on June 5th, 2002 (RT I 2002, 55, 345), amended by (RT I 2003,1,3). Available at <www.riigiteataja.ee/ert/act.jsp?id=241458>. Unofficial translation at <www.legaltext.ee/andmebaas/ava.asp?m=022>
- Võlaõigusseadus. Passed on 26 September 2001 (RT I 2001, 81, 487),

Interview

- Personal interview with sales coordination manager Maxim Afanasjev on 5 November 2004 on the practices employed by TECO Lines AS regarding procedure of obtaining a bill of lading and other issues.

Appendix

Printed in Great Britain
by Amazon